PIERCING the VEIL

EXAMINING **SAN DIEGO'S HAUNTED** HISTORY

CHARLES L. SPRATLEY

Schiffer Publishing Ltd
4880 Lower Valley Road • Atglen, PA 19310

Schiffer Books are available at special discounts for bulk purchases for sales promotions or premiums. Special editions, including personalized covers, corporate imprints, and excerpts can be created in large quantities for special needs. For more information contact the publisher:

Published by Schiffer Publishing, Ltd.
4880 Lower Valley Road
Atglen, PA 19310
Phone: (610) 593-1777; Fax: (610) 593-2002
E-mail: Info@schifferbooks.com

For the largest selection of fine reference books on this and related subjects, please visit our website at
www.schifferbooks.com
We are always looking for people to write books on new and related subjects. If you have an idea for a book, please contact us at
proposals@schifferbooks.com

This book may be purchased from the publisher.
Please try your bookstore first.
You may write for a free catalog.

In Europe, Schiffer books are distributed by
Bushwood Books
6 Marksbury Ave.
Kew Gardens
Surrey TW9 4JF England
Phone: 44 (0) 20 8392 8585; Fax: 44 (0) 20 8392 9876
E-mail: info@bushwoodbooks.co.uk
Website: www.bushwoodbooks.co.uk

Library of Congress Control Number: 2012942701

Designed by RoS
Type set in Trajan Pro/Calibri

ISBN: 978-0-7643-4140-3
Printed in The United States of America

CONTENTS

PREFACE

BY MOLLY MCCLAIN,
UNIVERSITY OF SAN DIEGO

Not all ghost stories take place in haunted castles or old New England houses.

The American West produced hundred of ghosts, from heartbroken lovers in frontier towns to desiccated '49ers still looking for gold. Their stories have become interwoven with history, making it particularly important to separate fact from fiction. Hence the aim of this book.

In *Piercing the Veil: Examining San Diego's Haunted History,* author Charles Spratley looks for the true stories behind legends that linger in Southern California. A former museum curator and ghost-tour operator, he has spent years unearthing the facts about apparitions and paranormal activity in the greater San Diego region, including the Bay, Old Town, the Gaslamp District, Coronado, Julian, and the Anza-Borrego Desert. He explains the context in which nineteenth-century Americans began to tell ghost stories; he also considers the continued presence of spectral figures in the modern age.

Ghosts still walk among us, even in a modern city like San Diego with its freeways, shopping malls, and suburbs. Not all readers "feel" the presence of the supernatural; but, with the help of this thoughtful book, they will better understand the human stories that these sites contain.

~MOLLY MCCLAIN
PROFESSOR, HISTORY DEPARTMENT
UNIVERSITY OF SAN DIEGO

If you are interested in the paranormal, I strongly recommend reading Jay Anson's book purely for its entertainment value. You will find it full of inconsistencies with plot lines concocted to possibly make the story flow. Even the priest that the Lutz family contacted, Father Pecoraro, could not be pinned down to tell the truth. His comments on the matter flip-flopped as the years went by, and when asked to give a legal affidavit on the haunting, he claimed to only have had limited contact with the Lutzes, and most of that was by phone. The book, I believe, is a work of fiction.

So, from where did the story come? William Weber, Ronald DeFeo Jr.'s lawyer. In a *People* magazine interview, in 1979, he admitted that he concocted the story with the Lutzes over "a few bottles of wine" in hopes of securing his client a new trial with an insanity plea. Shortly after that news broke, there was a huge lawsuit between Weber and the Lutzes that involved several others. Even *Good Housekeeping* magazine was dragged into the fray for an article they wrote about the infamous haunting. In the end, people got sued, no one really won, the Lutzes divorced, and the house was sold at an inflated price.

But despite the confession, the legend continues. In the DVD extras of the 2005 remake, actress Melissa George, who portrays Kathy Lutz, proclaims that one of the reasons she chose to do the movie was because it had been "based on a true story." That's Hollywood for you. Never let the facts get in the way of a good story, indeed.

Another example is a beautiful old Elk's Lodge that's part of my haunted tour of Old Towne Orange. I have never disputed the fact that the place may have supernatural activity. Like Harry Houdini, I honestly hope that there is life beyond the grave and constantly search for some evidence towards that. When someone says they experienced something, I believe that they experienced *something*, and try not to form any judgment about their integrity or sanity.

My primary issue is when they try to explain the haunting. I have interviewed the owner of the antiques store that operates on the street level of the lodge several times. The story he tells is that during World War II, Nazi prisoners were held in the basement if they misbehaved or were belligerent while they worked the local citrus fields as prisoners of war.

When I first heard the story, I was skeptical and went to the local Orange History Center and looked up records for that building. I perused the entire history of the building, including the war years, and could find no evidence indicating that the basement was ever used as a prison for naughty Nazis. In fact, I discovered that the Lodge was used by American servicemen in World War II as a billet while they were training in the nearby desert preparing for war, probably in Africa. I found newspaper articles and local history books that covered the town of Orange during the war years, and nowhere can I find anything about German POWs. I read about the local Japanese families sent off to internment camps and Boy Scouts holding newspaper and scrap metal drives while burning effigies of Hitler on a noose, but nothing of U-boat officers in the basement of a prominent building.

Where did the story come from? I honestly don't know, but can only follow logic and give it my best guess. Most of the local area was originally founded in the 1860s by farmers, German farmers. In fact, the neighboring town next to Orange is Anaheim, the home of Disneyland. Anaheim is actually a German name, the first part, *Ana*, is named after the local River, the Santa Ana River. *Heim*, is the German equivalent to the English word "home." I have also found evidence of Orange being settled in the same way. The architecture, the churches in the area, the place names, all point to a heavy Germanic influence.

What is a more plausible answer? Perhaps young boys, not old enough to fight in the war, were forced to work the fields and heard German spoken by the old men who labored beside them. Or that the U.S. caught German prisoners off the coast, made them work in the fields, and held them prisoner in a basement. If they were captured off the East Coast, would they be transported all the way across the country just for cheap labor?

An *LA Times* article, April 12, 2004, reports that Dennis Leslie, an avid World War II buff and historian, stated that German POWs were housed in Garden Grove and sent to work the fields in the area. Statements from article:

> ...brought to United States via Queen Mary and then shipped across U.S. via Pullman Cars. The POW camp was located at what is now Garden Grove Boulevard and Palm, no sign that camp was ever there. German POWs in California represented 10% of wartime workforce that included 75,000 migrant Mexican, 1600 Jamaicans, undetermined Chinese.

One article from *Garden Grove News*, covers the camp. In March 16, 1945:

> Residents of the district need have no fear of the prisoners. They...are not of the dangerous type but rather are men who were farm workers at home who would rather be working here than idle behind barb wire.

Camp was setup in 1945 by Citrus Growers Inc. 600 arrived in 1945, 500 in 1946. Men were docile and polite. Worked to make their quota and then spent the day learning English, dancing, performing plays, etc. Some even came back after the war to live in the area.

The Historical Society advised that they may have been used as "slave labor" at the citrus groves in 1945; then, after the war, they moved them to Santa Ana Airbase for continued labor and incarceration till the end of 1946. By all accounts they were treated very well with their own store and medical services.

I have since heard stories repeated by others, and they mostly go back to men who grew up in Orange--a "friend of a friend" style of analogy. When I toured the basement and was shown the "jail" where they were supposedly kept, I was shown where the iron door was attached to the cement wall. Honestly, all I saw was some broken cement with some rebar sticking out. No sign of hinges or casements for mounting a door, even a makeshift one. But the owner didn't want to hear that, either.

So many times I have investigated a famous haunted location, read the stories, spoken to the locals then started to delve into history for its origins. Unfortunately, it seems that some of these stories are the products of rent-a-psychics, public relations machines, and industrious business owners. It doesn't help when the National Trust for Historic Preservation encourages ghost stories at historic sites to help visitors to feel more personally connected to the building's history. In a 2001 newsletter, it stated, "We should celebrate any ghost stories that make the past more vivid and compelling for others" in an article by Byrd Wood entitled *Haunted Houses: Preservation Help or Horror.* The National Trust for Historic Preservation has even offered a session on "Paranormal Promotions" at its annual conference. But the true reality and history of these haunted places is usually far more fascinating and equally titillating without all the smoke and mirrors, exaggerations and downright fabrications to make a buck.

I have been called a skeptic, and I am comfortable with that. Skepticism is about inquiry, doubt, and examination on both sides of an issue. History isn't foolproof—after all, it is written by men, if it's even recorded at all. For example, during the early years of California statehood and the mass emigration, very little was recorded except for in a few towns such as San Diego, San Francisco, and Los Angeles which had regular newspapers. Most of early California's history was handed down through storytelling, usually secondhand accounts and sometimes many years after the event had occurred.

In the absence of tangible written accounts, the investigation of the paranormal often requires us to rely heavily on these stories. But historic ghost stories typically fall into one of two categories: folklore and legends, and fakelore. Folklore and legends usually originate from oral histories passed down over time until put in a written form. Fakelore, a term coined in 1950 by folklore professor Richard Dorson, is often misleading or embellished history that is presented as fact. When delving into the history of a ghostly presence, the back story or reason for the activity usually falls into one of these categories. Needless to say, fakelore poses the greatest threat to the preservation of history.

We can turn to old newspapers for some research, but during the time of the dime novels in the mid-1800s, these stories became sensationalized in order to sell- the precursor to what would later become known as yellow journalism, the Victorian tabloid media. In time, governments and courts were established, which created a recorded history of crimes, testimony, and coroners' inquests. Census records can tell us who lived where and when, while genealogical sites can be a valuable source of immigration records and more.

But as rewarding as it is when we find an old newspaper article or diary entry that relates a historic event, sometimes it's not what you find, but what you don't. Absence of evidence is just as important in construing a backstory. The danger is when someone interprets or makes assumptions, and then presents it as fact when, in reality, it's just become fakelore. Details about an event should become more scant and vague as time goes by, not more specific. As you'll soon see, most ghost stories have snowballed into a contrived history. Names, actions, and even dialogue have been added over the years to make it sound more authentic, but these details have absolutely no supporting evidence, and sadly, many of these details surfaced post 1960.

Today's technology-driven, Internet-dominant culture has given us access to more information than ever before; it's literally at our fingertips. We can put names, places, and events into search engines and receive thousands of results on a singular subject. For a historian, there's a tremendous amount of information that can be gathered with a few keystrokes, as opposed to spending hours in a local library scanning through microfilm, books, or tracking down old periodicals. Many historic newspapers are now available online, so an armchair historian can search through recorded history from the comfort of a home office.

But the technology is a double-edged sword. This easy access to information is a conduit to laziness and gullibility. People search the web for a famous house or ghost story and automatically assume that what they find must be true... It's on the Internet, after all. So they regurgitate these stories as fact, whether it's on the Internet, in a book, on a ghost tour, or in a magazine article, and believe that they have thoroughly done their research. But it's not enough to "Google" something in order to meet the burden of proof. In an age when reality TV is more scripted than real, we need to question what we find, roll up our sleeves, go back to basics, and hit the library, museum, and local historical societies.

Using my love for ghost stories, my knack as a historian, and my beliefs in critical thinking, I have compiled this volume filled to the brim with real history and the macabre. I want to delve past most regional haunting books that simply retell myth and legend and sell them as fact. I want to go beyond all the Internet sites that seem to repeat the same information over and over. History is an onion, and the layers must be peeled back.

Come with me, dear readers, let us *Pierce the Veil.*

CHAPTER ONE

UNDERSTANDING THE PARANORMAL

In order to try and understand the paranormal world around us, first we must delve into its origins. From the beginning of time, man has been fascinated with the Otherworld. There are Biblical references to communicating with spirits, as well as references to ghosts in early literature. Examining the entire history of that alone would be a book in itself.

Paranormal investigation, as we can understand it, really came about in the early Victorian age. From 1837 to 1901, it was an era of new thought and industry. Machines were invented to replace men in the workplace, handmade goods were able to be mass-produced, and the invention of photography, railroads, electricity, and improvements in communication and medicine also dramatically changed everyday life. Along with these technological advances, came a desire for a more lavish and opulent lifestyle—fancy clothing, ornate home decor, delicate architecture. It became a fine line between gentility and brutality.

The expansion of the British Empire exposed the world to new philosophies and religions, which were then brought back for discussion and study. In 1859, Charles Darwin published *The Origin of Species* and forever changed the way people thought about themselves and the world around them. Darwin and his theories on evolution had created doubt in people's minds of blind faith. If man was descended from apes and our current form is merely a freak byproduct of natural selection, then what are we? What is God? The world was ripe for the paranormal.

Science was explaining away some of man's previously-held beliefs and mysteries. People were looking for a new movement, an inspiration for their weary souls and they found it in the séance.

Contacting the spirit of a dead peddler, two sisters became instant celebrities and brought about the birth of modern-day Spiritualism. The Fox sisters, Kate and Margaret, the two youngest of three, allegedly began communicating with a spirit in the form of rappings. They referred to the spirit as "Mr. Splitfoot," which is a nickname for the Devil. The home the family moved into had some prior history of being haunted, but the Fox family had lived there for some time before communication with the spirit was supposedly established.

According to Margaret's autobiography, written in 1888, her attempts at intelligent conversation with the spirit, using the rappings as the means of communications, began in 1848. There was a series setup, using the number of raps to designate letters, numbers, etc. You can only imagine what a slow process this must have been to get out lengthy sentences. Through these rappings, they determined that the spirit was that of a murdered peddler whose body was buried in the cellar. Indeed, a body was eventually discovered in the cellar in 1904.

The Fox sisters became instant celebrities in their small community in Wayne County, New York. When they eventually separated in Rochester, the rappings apparently followed them. Meeting with friends of the family, the Fox sisters soon became involved with a radical Quaker group that was convinced that they were the real deal. This group of Quakers later evolved into the first group of Spiritualists and, like wildfire, their influence and ideals would spread across the globe.

Sadly though, the young ladies were pushed beyond their limits and fell to alcoholism and constant ridicule. Margaret confessed that it was all a fraud, and that she was able to crack her knuckles and joints to produce the sounds, and the sitters present would let their overactive imaginations do the rest. Margaret recanted her confession in 1889, and both sisters died in poverty within a few years. Kate, though shocked by her sister's letters and attacks on Spiritualism, which was at the height of its popularity by then, never spoke an ill word about Margaret. The Fox sisters took the secret of their spectral communication to the grave.

By the mid-nineteenth century, Spiritualism had established its own churches and "home circles," where groups of people would congregate to conduct table tipping, rappings, or other similar phenomena. The traditional form of rappings, as devised by the Fox sisters, must have been quite tedious; however, because soon after the Spiritualism movement started in New York and made its way to Europe, new devices and techniques were developed. This is, after all, the Victorian era, an age of invention and innovation.

The medium, or person who would try to communicate with the dead within a group, often attempted something called automatic writing. A pencil was placed in the medium's hand and the medium allowed the spirit in question to move the pencil to its will. But that also seemed to prove too time consuming, so a basket, and later a small piece of wood, was attached to the pencil, providing a better grip for the medium. This innovation is believed to have given birth to the planchette which was used in conjunction with the Ouija board. The Ouija board, patented in 1890, is probably the only recognizable remnant of the Victorian Spiritualist movement, and you have Parker Brothers to thank for it.

A great number of prominent people began to take an interest in Spiritualism, including W.B. Yeats, Ezra Pound, Wassily Kandinsky, Piet Mondrian, Marcel Duchamp, Max Ernst, Arthur Conan Doyle, and Sigmund Freud, who declared in a letter written in 1921:

> If I had my life to live over again, I should devote my life to psychical research rather than psychoanalysis.

While it seems natural that artists and writers would find Spiritualism so compelling, the movement also began to attract scientists. Some of these scientists, namely psychiatrists and physicists, were increasingly interested in the new paranormal phenomena. Probably the most famous of these was William Crookes, whom some consider to be the father of ghost hunting. He investigated the likes of D.D. Home, Kate Fox, and Florence Cook (whom it was later revealed he may have had an amorous affair with). If a medium claimed to produce something, there was a scientist, or *investigator* as they liked to be called, there to call them on it. The line in the sand had been drawn.

While some in the scientific community sought to explain it, others scoffed at it, calling it a pseudoscience at best. Probably one of the famous opponents of fake mediums was none other than the stage magician, Harry Houdini. He would travel to séances around the country, sometimes in disguise, and expose the fakes, but not because he didn't believe in the paranormal. Rather, Houdini was desperate to establish communication with the Other Side and spent time and effort searching for a capable conduit. He gave lectures on how mediums worked and was even one of the members of the board for *Scientific American*.

There was a drop-off in the interest of the paranormal during the 1930s until the 1960s. It still existed, but went from the living room to the basement if you will. I have a theory on its resurgence at this time: Life imitates art. During the late 1960s and early 1970s came a flurry of films about the occult—*Rosemary's Baby, The Exorcist, The Amityville Horror*, just to name a few, along with television shows such as *In Search Of...* Interest in the paranormal, as well as the investigation of it, grew...along with the ghost stories themselves.

From this rediscovery came paranormal investigators such as Hans Holzer, whom many in the field call the original modern ghost hunter (though my methods or research are very different, I have respect for him for bringing the science back to life).

On the other side of the field were people like Mario Truzzi, a sociology professor who, upon the reading of his works, changed the way I look at the paranormal. He believed and preached a philosophy known as zeteticism, and its most basic tenet is: "Extraordinary claims require extraordinary proof." Truzzi founded CSICOP (Committee for the Scientific Investigation of Claims of the Paranormal) in 1978, but later left it because he felt that the committee wasn't giving the paranormal the fair shot he felt it deserved. He was the skeptic's skeptic.

But skepticism is grossly misunderstood. Skepticism is about inquiry, doubt and examination of both sides of an issue. The origins and basis of modern skepticism have been defined by CSICOP. These include the Burden of Proof (the principle that if a paranormal claim is made, it is up to the claimant to substantiate it: non-believers do not need to refute it), Occam's Razor (that explanations should be as simple as possible) and Sagan's Balance (this is the principle that extraordinary claims require extraordinary evidence). This was contrasted with older versions of skepticism, such as those of the ancient Greeks, which had different goals.

In the arguments of philosophers such as British mathematician W. K. Clifford and, more recently, Professor Jonathan Adler, it is unethical to hold beliefs which are not supported by evidence. In 1879, Clifford stated, "The danger to society is not merely that it should believe wrong things, though that is great enough; but that it should become credulous, and lose the habit of testing things and inquiring of them; for then it must sink back into savagery." This is directly relevant to skepticism since, by its very definition, the paranormal is not adequately supported by evidence. Thus, the arguments of Clifford and Adler suggest that skepticism is an ethical approach, as well as an intellectual one.

In the new Millennium, ghost stories grew increasingly popular, paranormal activity ran wild until society was "rescued" by the SyFy Channel and two guys who work for Roto-Rooter. In 2004, "Ghost Hunters" took to the small screen and gave a rather painful birth to the amateur paranormal investigator. Groups sprang up all over the world to mimic this duo who investigates the Other Side when not occupied discovering what clogged up your drains. They carry a veritable Best Buy electronic collection in their vans and set up an impressive array of cameras and sensors in hopes of collecting "evidence".

There are shows that try to be more circumspect when investigating the paranormal. First they see a submitted video, which never fails to astound them. Then they go out to the place where it allegedly occurred and try to investigate it by replicating the phenomena using modern photographic and special effect techniques. They almost always get "stumped" when they investigate hauntings and the paranormal. When they can't replicate something, they usually declare it authentic. Maybe instead of a photographer or a special effects guy, they should have brought in a stage magician or an illusionist to set things right. A good psychiatrist would also do wonders for their team.

A skeptic is someone who seeks the truth but most investigators usually don't look deep or very far. The truly sad part about one group of reality television ghost investigators is that they have been accused of using falsified footage. If the submitted video isn't fantastical enough, the originators are asked to reshoot it to fit the bill and usually receive a hefty fee for their trouble—another reality show that is anything but. Sometimes I feel like I'm in the wrong business—I could make a killing creating creepy videos to send in for someone to debunk or justify all in the name of good TV.

Just how do we detect paranormal activity today? The most basic form of detection is photography. Some of the best potential evidence of a haunting has been captured on film. Second is a recording of sound, an Electronic Voice Phenomenon, or EVP. It is believed that a spirit may communicate but may be too quiet or at a range that our human ears cannot pick up. Recordings taken at a site are filtered through a computer in hope of finding some proof of paranormal activity. I have issues with EVP, for I feel that the software used can distort the sound. It only takes someone who *wants* to hear ghosts to detect ghosts, or at least their imagination will.

There are also thermometers for measuring changes in room temperature and EMF detectors that measure electromagnetic interference in an area. I'm still trying to make a judgment on EMF detectors. Shows such as "Ghost Hunters" are very careful to say the word "theory" before they claim what the EMF detector does. There is no scientific proof that an EMF reader detects anything other than normal readings in nature or artificially generated.

All of these tools can be helpful in investigating an alleged haunting, but they all have their own pitfalls as well. In all my years of metal and woodworking, let me just say this: The tool is only as good as the person wielding it.

Last, but hardly least, the professional psychic found a new realm to explore. No longer relegated to reading Tarot cards or tea leaves, they usually join these paranormal investigative teams in some facet and attempt to help them in their research. Unfortunately, psychics typically offer unsubstantiated or unverifiable claims or produce information that is already known. Usually, psychics only add to the body count without any evidence that these ghosts had a human counterpart.

Psychics often make numerous claims of apparitions and identities, hoping that people will recognize some and ignore or misinterpret the wrong ones. Hans Holzer, the self-proclaimed "world's leading expert on haunted houses," frequently relied on psychics when conducting his paranormal investigations, including "witch" Sybil Leek (1922-1982). Her investigations of haunted sites across the country produced more misses than hits. Holzer's explanation for this was that the places simply had undiscovered spirits.

Psychics have been said by some to be one of the most dangerous threats to the preservation of history. They have been known to create people who never existed, crimes or events that never took place, or motives that can alter a family's heritage. Oftentimes, there are plenty of the "usual suspects" in a haunted place—people die in hotels, in private homes, or in public places. But psychics are often given the power to create a person and then give that individual a history and motive for remaining on the haunted site—many without benefit of a death certificate. People then swallow this up as part of their city's history. As you'll learn, the origins of some very famous hauntings are not the result of an actual death on the premises, but rather a psychic impression.

What constitutes a haunting? There is much debate out there on the subject and opinions vary, but a general consensus has been reached over the years. There are several types of hauntings: Ghosts, spirits, poltergeists, and what I will simply label as *other.* Ghosts themselves can be very common. They are also referred to as a residual haunt, a "recording" in time. The ghost will perform the same action over and over again. They are not sentient and completely harmless.

A spirit though, is a completely different ball of wax. It is sentient. It may try to interact or it may completely choose to ignore you or its surroundings. I have even read reports of people communicating with a person, only to find out that the person has been dead for some time.

The idea that a ghost is almost always visible and usually light blue or translucent is sheer Hollywood. The chance of seeing a full-bodied apparition is extremely slim. You can consider yourself blessed if you can hear or smell them in your presence.

Poltergeists are unusual. From the German word meaning "noisy ghost," a Poltergeist may be one of two things. Some believe that it may be a spirit strong enough to move objects, or it may even be a form of subconscious telekinesis on the part of its "victim." Some attribute Poltergeist activity to the overactive imagination of pre-teen girls who are usually most affected by this.

Other typical paranormal experiences include cold spots, tugging on hair or clothing, flickering lights or other electrical disturbances (such as batteries being drained), a general feeling of malaise or dread, the detection of movement or air swooshing by, peripheral sightings, mist and, my personal favorite, orbs. Orbs are bright spots that appear in photography which some believe indicate spirits floating in air. However, it should be noted that photography experts are pretty much unanimous in identifying orbs as merely dust particles or precipitation in the air. It is interesting to note that orbs only appear on digital cameras, not film cameras.

One thing every haunting has in common: It starts with a dead body. You can't have a spirit without a human counterpart. As some haunted places gain notoriety, paranormal experiences begin to rack up and the body count surges. According to Joe Nickell, author and senior research fellow of CSICOP, one lodge near Santa Cruz, California invited a very famous psychic to investigate its paranormal activity. The psychic envisioned a girl named "Sara" and brought the total number of entities "detected" at the lodge to forty-nine. Odds are that forty-nine different people did not die on the premises.

Old buildings, graveyards, and historic homes not only have a past, they have a soul, and some people are more sensitive and better able to connect with a site. For example, whenever I step inside the old jailhouse in historic Julian, I sense something strange, a vibe or feeling that something isn't right. There is something otherworldly there, although I've never seen anything tangible. It's a sixth sense. My colleague, on the other hand, just gets the urge to sweep the floors and clean the place.

Perhaps this is what the late University of Kentucky professor emeritus Robert A. Baker meant when he said,

> There are no haunted places, only haunted people.

CHAPTER TWO

THE HISTORY OF SAN DIEGO

It is important to become briefly familiar with the history of San Diego and how it developed into a city before examining its haunted history. One must learn how and where the city became occupied in order to apply the historic claims as they pertain to the paranormal. Know the history, and you get a better understanding of the ghost stories.

Originally settled by Native Americans of the Kumeyaay tribe, the first European explorers were Spanish, but no Europeans settled in this area until 1769, when Fra Junipero Serra finally received his orders from Spain to create and oversee a string of missions in Alta, California. These missions, especially the one in San Diego, were more fort-like in construction. Every mission was situated approximately one day's travel by horseback away, so that an efficient form of communication could be set up. It is believed by many historians that the mission system was actually established as a way to lay claim to Alta, California, in order to prevent it from being claimed by Russia, who was attempting to make its way south from Alaska. The first mission and Presidio (Spanish for *fort*) was built on a hill overlooking the harbor and was occupied by settlers and soldiers for many years, protecting this newly acquired piece of the Spanish Empire.

In 1774, a new, larger mission was built a few miles inland along the San Diego River. Perhaps the priests felt they no longer needed military protection from the Native Americans in the area. Sadly, they were wrong. Shortly after the mission was built, it was attacked one night by some angry locals and a priest was killed. A fire broke out which caused significant damage. It took quite awhile for the unprotected Mission to gain the respect and trust of the nearby tribes. This officially became known as Mission San Diego de Alcala and it still stands to this day, the first of the California Missions.

After Mexico seceded from Spain, the Presidio practically became obsolete. By the 1820s, a small pueblo started at the bottom of the hill from the old fort. Roof tiles were salvaged from the fortifications and used on some of the new homes. Soon, the majestic Presidio was a memory, falling into complete disrepair. The small pueblo became what we now know as Old Town San Diego. No longer under a military occupation, the town was ruled by an Alcalde under a mayoral system. In May 1846, the U.S. declared war on Mexico.

On July 30, 1846, Commodore Robert F. Stockton took charge of a sloop-of-war, *Cyane,* and along with 160 men under Lt. John C. Fremont, landed in San Diego Harbor and raised the American flag in the plaza of the pueblo of San Diego. They received no resistance from the Californios, land owners of Spanish-speaking Catholic descent born in what is now California. Many of their daughters had married American military officers and they knew that Mexico probably couldn't hold California forever.

In December of 1846, the Army of the West, led by General Stephen Watts Kearny, fought a brief battle against General Andres Pico and his Mexican-California army for control of California, which almost ended in disaster. Miscalculations, rainy weather, and underestimating the enemy resulted in the loss of twenty-two Americans and eleven Mexicans. Although the war was eventually won by the U.S., it was considered an important victory for the Californios. The Treaty of Guadalupe Hidalgo was later signed in 1848, just a month after gold was discovered at Sutter's Mill, which ended the war with Mexico and established the boundary between the U.S. and Mexico.

By the early 1850s, San Diego resembled many western towns with about 100 houses and 700 inhabitants. A few wooden buildings were scattered amongst the adobe structures of the town's earlier occupants. Most of the buildings framed a large dirt plaza which was the center of public life and recreation in the town. Certain times of the year, such as Sundays and holidays, the citizens enjoyed such sports as bull and bear encounters, bullfighting, horse races, and bear baiting. In a letter to his mother, merchant Thomas Whaley described the town as "a dreary place, the inhabitants of which many of them are from the rough-scruff of creation."

Most early San Diegans, like Whaley, stuck it out in the dusty town and pinned their hopes on the arrival of the railroad to connect San Diego with the East. But San Diego was bypassed after numerous expeditions and surveys and the railroad wouldn't arrive for another thirty years. William Heath Davis attempted to establish a New Town closer to the waterfront, buying up lots and building a home, but an economic depression put a halt to that, and by 1853, most buildings were moved back to Old Town.

Things didn't pick up in San Diego until after the end of the Civil War. In 1867, an ambitious young man named Alonzo Horton arrived in San Diego and began buying land closer to a natural harbor that was situated a couple miles to the south of San Diego. Over the next couple of years, he built a wharf, a bank, and a luxurious hotel in what was then known as New Town and quickly became the center of activity for San Diego. The old pueblo at the bottom of the hill from the Presidio became vacant as residents moved to the new city center.

When gold was discovered in the local mountains in 1869, thousands of people began migrating to the area, which is now the historic part of downtown San Diego, the Gaslamp Quarter. Between the new shipping port, the bustling harbor, and the arrival of the railroad, San Diego became one of the busiest towns on the West Coast. All walks of life strolled the streets of San Diego. Wealthy benefactors rubbed elbows with gamblers and prostitutes. The population of San Diego hit its peak at 40,000 during the 1880s with a widespread real estate boom.

In the 1890s though, San Diego suffered a huge economic depression led by a Wall Street panic in 1893. Businesses closed while people went elsewhere looking for work. The population plummeted down to 17,000. But by the turn of the century, new social reforms across America raised San Diego back up to its former glory. In 1907, the U.S. Navy's Great White Fleet, on a fourteen-month circumnavigation of the world in a mission to demonstrate the Navy's capability, made its first U.S. stop in San Diego bringing more than 16,000 sailors into San Diego Harbor on 16 battleships, 7 destroyers, and 4 auxiliary ships. San Diego became one of the most popular ports for sailors with the creation of the Stingaree District.

San Diego expanded in all directions. The occasional Victorian mansion sprang up amongst middle class homes to the east of New Town in areas now known as Sherman Heights and Golden Hill. To the north, Old Town crumbled while the community of Mission Hills above it flourished and grew. In the southern part of San Diego, agriculture became a staple and for the wealthy, the Hotel del Coronado was a ferry ride away to the southwest of New Town.

San Diego blossomed with the coming of the Panama-California Exposition of 1915-1916 and the development of Balboa Park, the nation's largest urban cultural park. As the host location for two world fairs, the park became home to fifteen major museums, beautiful gardens, and the San Diego Zoo.

Congressman William Kettner secured the necessary federal funding to have the San Diego Bay dredged so that deep-draft ships could enter. Not only was the depth of the bay increased for military, as well as civilian and merchant shipping, but the dredged soil was used to expand the coastline. San Diego became the site of the largest naval fleet in the world with the largest concentration of naval facilities worldwide and became a real economic powerhouse of the west, rivaling cities such as Los Angeles and San Francisco.

Today, San Diego is California's second largest city and the eighth largest in the U.S. It's famous for its idyllic climate, miles of beaches, and attractions. Whether you are visiting San Diego, are a resident, or truly blessed and a native like me, this city is deep in history...and in its ghosts.

CHAPTER THREE

AMERICA'S MOST HAUNTED?

THE WHALEY HOUSE

The Whaley House, located in Old Town San Diego, has been called many things, but has earned notoriety for the tagline "America's Most Haunted." Hans Holzer, the famous ghost hunter from the 1960s and '70s, made the house internationally famous for its paranormal activity. He came to the house on June 25, 1965, with then-local television personality Regis Philbin and self-proclaimed witch and seer Sybil Leek . According to Hans Holzer's *Ghosts of the Golden West*, published in 1968, they experienced many things, including the ghosts of an executed man, Thomas and Anna Whaley, and a little girl. Philbin's own encounter with the ghost of Anna Whaley was described in an article that appeared in a 2001 edition of the *National Enquirer*, entitled "Regis: I Saw A Ghost With My Own Eyes." Holzer wrote about his experiences at the Whaley House and the testimonies of others in several of his books over his lifetime including his magnum opus aptly entitled *Ghosts.*

Every year, literally thousands of people visit the Whaley House to try and experience some kind of paranormal phenomena. Whenever the Whaley House comes up in conversation, people tell me a story of an orb in a photo or an experience a friend of theirs had. Everything from poltergeist activity in the form of swinging utensils in the kitchen to phantom footsteps to windows that open and close on their own to levitating furniture to full-blown apparitions are claimed to have been seen. I tried to get a count of the different ghosts encountered at the Whaley House, described in books and on the Internet, but stopped at forty-three—Thomas, Anna, a Native American woman, Sheriff McCoy, a workman, a young girl, dogs, cats, and so many more.

I myself have a personal stake in the stories, for I used to work at the Whaley House as a docent and guide. I have spent more time in that house as an employee than most paranormal investigators would dare dream of. America's Most Haunted, indeed. Even Save Our Heritage Organization (SOHO), the organization that acts as caretaker for the historic home, makes use of the claim, although it has the modesty of adding a question mark to the boast—America's Most Haunted? By the way, who claims that the Whaley House is the most actively haunted house in the United States? The Travel Channel.

CERTIFIED HAUNT?

One of the most prolific misconceptions about the Whaley House is that it is officially "certified haunted" by the United States Government or an "authentic haunted house," a fallacy that has continued throughout the years. When I first heard the story, I marveled at how easily the public swallowed it hook, line, and sinker. Every book and website that I originally turned to for research stated this. Only John Lamb, in his book *Spectral San Diego* raised questions to this fact, but he did not dig any deeper on the matter. He just wanted to know if the particular government agency that certified haunted houses had any job openings.

The truth was actually quite easy to uncover. In the 1970s, there was an attempt to boost tourism in the U.S. as part of a domestic tourism program supported by radio programs and publicity tours. The United States Travel Service (USTS), a subdivision of the U.S. Department of Commerce and now defunct, put together a packet of brochures on various subjects, one of them a listing of haunted houses. Actually, they sent out a request to different historic house museums and asked them if they offered a ghost tour or believed they were haunted, publishing the results for tourism purposes only. First, I started with local representatives at the U.S. Department of Commerce, then moved my way up the chain to the federal level. I found someone who was employed at the time by the USTS and remembered the travel brochures well. He explained that there was no checking up on the claims or verifications done, it was a tourism gimmick only, but was unbelievably popular.

I then discovered a *New York Times* article dated July 17, 1977, that covered the publishing of the brochure, entitled "Who's Whoooo! in America." The supernatural was hugely popular in the 1970s, with television shows such as *In Search Of...*, books and movies like *The Amityville Horror,* and *The Exorcist*. So you can easily imagine the popularity of a comprehensive guide to about thirty

Whaley House front porch.

Whaley House—back of house in yard.

"haunted houses" across the country. Visitation to such places as the Winchester House, Robert E. Lee's home, and, yes, the Whaley House, increased and they've been riding on that coat-tail ever since.

I recently watched in amazement on television when a paranormal group with a heavy emphasis on logic and science (according to their reputations) visited the Whaley House museum for a paranormal investigation and were told this mistruth by their guide, an employee of the museum. Websites and books from many "famous" paranormal investigators state this simply as fact when it is really incomplete research. There is no government agency that verifies or determines the authenticity of a haunted location. There was once a division of the U.S. Department of Commerce that promoted tourism from 1961-1996 and they developed programs to encourage tourism to U.S. destinations. So is the Whaley House certified as haunted by the U.S. Government? Hardly, but it makes great press.

THE STORY OF THOMAS WHALEY

The story of Thomas Whaley is an interesting one. He was a prolific letter writer and his personal papers have been used as a valuable resource for much of San Diego's early history. Following what was the dream of many, the California Gold Rush, he left his home in New York at the age of 26 and sailed 204 days around Cape Horn to San Francisco. After being there for two years, he followed financial advice from a friend and traveled to San Diego in October 1851. Learning Spanish so he could do business with the "natives" in the small pueblo, Thomas opened a store that dealt in general merchandise, a business that would dominate his career for better or for worse. In 1853, he returned to New York where he married Anna Louise DeLaunay and they promptly sailed back to San Diego to start their new life.

Over the next couple of years, the Whaleys moved at least twice, and their first child, Francis, was born late in 1854. Life couldn't have been easy for the newlyweds. Thomas' brother, Henry, came to San Diego as well and they started a new store together. They quarreled often and it was said that Henry was frequently drunk and would call Thomas out into the street to settle their disputes with their fists. Upon constant requests from their mother, Rachel, the brothers dissolved their business and personal relationship.

Purchasing a brick business from George Tebbetts was a turning point for the entrepreneur. He used his own company bricks to start the construction of the building, that is now known as the Whaley House, in June 1856, with the actual two-story house construction starting in September of that same year. It served as the family home, and Thomas tried to run his store from it, but it was too far away from the town center and he moved his business back to the Plaza. In 1858,

Notes: Who's Whoooo On the Ghost Circuit

By ROBERT J. DUNPHY

The United States Travel Service, the national tourism office which operates a toll-free telephone service to provide advice on getting around in America, is apparently trying to put travelers in touch with the world beyond as well. The agency has issued a comprehensive guide to haunted houses in the United States, a project that has inevitably been dubbed "Who's Whoooo in America."

The "guide to ghost hosts" lists two dozen haunted houses open to visitors from Maine to California and even includes a ship, the United States frigate Constellation in Baltimore Harbor. The ghost of a sailor who died in 1799 is said to haunt the Constellation, which is now a floating museum.

Another surprise entry in the guide is the White House in Washington, where the ghost of Abraham Lincoln is said to walk the hallowed halls in times of national crisis. And a few blocks down Pennsylvania Avenue in the nation's Capitol, the ghost of Pierre L'Enfant, the Frenchman who designed the city, is said to pace the floors waiting for Congress to pay him for his work.

For the free list of haunted houses, along with the admission prices and hours of operation—including some spooky candlelight evening tours—write the U.S.T.S. at the Department of Commerce, Washington, D.C. 20230.

Meanwhile, in a somewhat more earthly endeavor, the Travel Service has embarked on the second year of dispensing tourist information over its nationwide toll-free telephone network (800-243-2372 everywhere except Connecticut, where the number is 800-822-7611). In the first year of operations, the U.S.T.S. received 11,592 inquiries from travel agents and the general public on where to go and what to see in the United States. One of the six editors who answer inquiries at the Travel Information Center in Lakeville, Conn., the headquarters of the U.S.T.S. telephone network, said most of the questions deal with sightseeing attractions, accommodations, national parks and battlefields. The service operates from 9 A.M. to 8 P.M. (Eastern time) Mondays through Fridays.

In addition to the toll-free telephone service in the United States, the U.S.T.S. also operates similar phone outlets in Mexico City and Canada for travelers planning trips to this country. The numbers in Canada are: 604-732-3308 in Vancouver; 416-964-3094, Toronto; and 514-861-0481, Montreal.

In Mexico City the number is 905-566-4000.

FASHION AND PERFUME

A 16-day vacation package in France, billed as the Cognoscenti Holiday at $2,495 per person (not including air transportation), has been designed to take 30 "exclusive" participants behind the scenes of French fashion and perfume in September. Members of the tour will meet the owners and operators of such firms as Lanvin, Patou, Hermes and Guerlain and visit the birthplace of perfume in Grasse as well as making stops on the French Riviera and in Paris. Travel Concepts International, the organizer, said the program will include "a whirl of chic private dinners, luncheons and official receptions," plus visits to laboratories and workrooms and an escorted tour through the private apartment of the late Coco Chanel.

The "Cognoscenti Holiday" will run from Sept. 23 to Oct. 8. Details are available from T.C.I., 1361 Madison Avenue, New York 10028 (212-369-0941).

SKINNY-DIPPING

A national organization dedicated to the promotion of nude bathing, or "free" beaches where swimsuits are optional, has launched a campaign against Peeping Toms who frequent their precincts as sightseers or voyeurs rather than as active participants.

The organization, Free Beaches, wants to present the interlopers with this "non-membership" card:

HONORARY FREE BEACH

GAWKER

'gawk-\gȯk\ *n* [perh. alter. of obs. *gow* (to stare)]: to gape or stare stupidly — gawk-er *n*

"For those who will not join"

Free Beaches, whose slogan is "Nude is not lewd," has just issued the 1977 edition of its annual "Guide to Nude Beaches in North America," a 16-page tabloid listing 277 public areas in 39 states and three Canadian provinces where skinny-dipping is practiced. The sites include lakes, quarries, old swimming holes and ocean beaches on the Atlantic and the Pacific. The guide carries several maps detailing the routes into the most popular areas. A spokesman for Free Beaches said 50,000 copies of its guide were distributed last year.

In the 1977 listings, California leads the states with 50 nude bathing areas, and there are a dozen listed under Florida, 17 under Massachusetts and 17 under New York City-Long Island. In addition to the listings of clothing-optional beaches, the guide contains tips on the most effective suntan lotions to protect sensitive parts of the body from overexposure to the sun and provides the names of travel agents who conduct tours to nude beaches. (In New York, it's Promenade Travel, 30 East 42d Street, New York 10017.)

Copies of the guide are available by sending a large self-addressed, stamped envelope with at least a $1 donation to Free Beaches, P.O. Box 132, Oshkosh, Wis. 54901.

RIPOFFS ON THE ROAD

The American Automobile Association has warned motorists contemplating cross-country trips this summer that members' complaints indicate that many service stations have been bilking travelers "through malicious damage to the vehicle, fraud or intimidation." Specifically cited were stations along Interstate 75 in Georgia, where the A.A.A. said 122 complaints were received in the first five months of this year. Among the allegations were that service stations warned motorists that perfectly good tires, shock absorbers and batteries should be replaced immediately.

The best way to avoid being bilked by service stations, the A.A.A. suggested, is to have the car thoroughly inspected by a reliable mechanic before departing on a trip, making certain that lights, wipers, fan belts, hoses and tires are checked. If a person is in doubt about a diagnosis on the road,

Continued on Page 23

Leo Cullum

"My kid is trying to lower the illiteracy rate in the United States. He's going to Mexico."

The New York Times
Published: July 17, 1977

"Who's Whooo" *New York Times* article.

after the death of their infant son from scarlet fever and fire had destroyed his store, Thomas packed up his family and moved to San Francisco.

Three more children were born to Thomas and Anna while in San Francisco and Thomas worked as a U.S. Army Commissary storekeeper. But Thomas' superior officer, Major Kirkham, received requests for his dismissal due to "complaints to detriment of Department constantly made against Whaley in Washington." Thomas claimed his conduct had been honorable, but resigned to avoid dishonorable discharge. He then took a position as an issuing clerk with the Army, in charge of three government transports with stores in Alaska. He was later elected councilman of Sitka while Anna and the children remained in San Francisco.

Meanwhile, the brick house had a variety of tenants, but fell into disrepair, damaged by severe rains and earthquakes. It also became rat infested. Thomas moved back to San Diego in 1868, after a ten-year absence. The family later joined him after a major earthquake in San Francisco, but Thomas left again, this time for New York, in 1873, and he didn't return until 1879.

In 1882, two of Thomas' daughters held a double wedding at the house. Violet married George Bertolacci while Anna married her first cousin, John Whaley. But by the following year, 22-year old Violet was granted a divorce after George deserted her after only two weeks of marriage. Despondent and humiliated, Violet committed suicide on August 19, 1885, by shooting herself in the heart with her father's 32-calibre Smith & Wesson pistol while in the privy. There was a coroner's inquest which included testimony from her sister, Corinne, and Thomas. Violet had made a half-hearted attempt at suicide the previous month by jumping into a cistern, but had second thoughts and screamed for help. Buried at Mt. Hope Cemetery, Violet left a suicide note which read:

> Mad from life's history, swift to death's mystery; glad to be hurled, anywhere, anywhere out of this world.

Grief-stricken, Thomas began building a house in New Town at 933 State Street and the family moved there. Thomas opened a real estate office nearby, but retired in 1888 due to ill health. He passed away at the New Town home on December 14, 1890 at the age of 67. His daughter, Anna, died in Modesto, California in 1905. The family remained in New Town until 1912 when they returned to the Whaley House. Several members died in the house, including Anna in 1913 and son, Francis, the following year.

Corinne Whaley, Thomas' last surviving child, lived in the house until November 1952. After her death in a Lemon Grove rest home the following year, the historic building was slated for demolition. June Reading, a former restaurant owner, fell in love with the house. Through the San Diego Historical

Shrine Foundation, she led the restoration and reopened the Whaley House as a museum for public tours in 1960. According to her January 27, 1998 obituary in the *San Diego Union*, Reading played a large part in perpetuating the notion that the Whaley House was haunted, "the better to promote Halloween evening tours."

GHOST STORIES

There are many famous ghost stories associated with the Whaley House and they all seem to stem from early 1960s articles in the *San Diego Union* from Mrs. Reading. The first time the Whaley house is mentioned as haunted is in an article dated November 10, 1961. It was in this article that Reading first mentions Yankee Jim Robinson, a boat thief who was hanged in 1852 from a large tree on the Whaley House site. According to Reading:

> The arch between the music room and parlor is over the tree's dead roots.

She also talked about hearing the footsteps of Yankee Jim during restoration.

It was in this article that we first heard of Corinne Lillian Whaley (from journals that no one has ever seen) and her belief in ghosts. She wrote:

> Signoret House was the scene of ghostly excitement for many nights. A spirit appeared as a shadowy figure and the only way they could scare it off was with the firing of a gun from a member of the crowd that would gather outside the house.

Oddly, this story only appeared once and never again. There is nothing to indicate that the Whaley House was ever referred to as Signoret House, so it's unknown what she was referring to. There was a Signoret House in Los Angeles, built for Felix Signoret during the 1870-'80s, which was also made of bricks in classic Victorian architecture, so unless her journals appear for verification, there's nothing to support the idea that she was talking about the Whaley House.

Over the next few years, several more articles were published in the *San Diego Union*. In April 1962, the California Parapsychology Foundation attempted to record phenomena at the Whaley House under the watchful eye of June Reading, but nothing unusual happened. Kay Sterner, president of the foundation, reported "seeing psychically" some of the residents, including a rather stocky man with a long whip in his hand, and two women, one with a straight-edge razor. The week before, Sterner had brought in Patrick Mahoney, an Irish psychophysicist and author who picked up on the death of a small child.

But in July 1962, the Parapsychology Research Foundation "drew two conclusions from its attempt to record ghostly sounds at the house. Either you can't record ghostly sounds or there weren't any ghosts there making sounds." But several persons present did report psychic impressions of ghosts. Milton Ferris, executive secretary, concluded:

> Unless we can measure something one way or another, any sounds or sights are just someone's impressions. As far as we're concerned, there's nothing there yet.

Until the famous Hans Holzer came to town and visited the Whaley House in 1965. He was greeted by Kay Sterner, and along with television personality Regis Philbin and English medium Sybil Leek, they dined together before going to the Whaley House to investigate. According to Holzer, he wasn't told anything about the history of the house, but knew only what he had read in a psychic newspaper called *Cosmic Star* in 1963. He claimed in a *San Diego Union* article on June 27, 1965, that Leek had "made contact and given us valuable evidence about the Whaley House she couldn't possibly have known beforehand."

In 1968, Holzer described his experience at the Whaley House in *Ghosts of the Golden West*. In the first chapter, he describes a few of the impressions given by others, including a small woman with a swarthy complexion wearing a cap, a man dressed in a frock coat and pantaloons, a dark-haired woman wearing a green-plaid gingham dress, and a spotted dog, "like a fox terrier." Most of these accounts were provided by employees/guides who worked at the Whaley House.

In a trance, Leek felt the presence of at least four ghosts, including one of a long-haired girl named Anna Bell who died of poisoning in 1872. There was a 32-year-old man, about 5'10", named Calstrop with a mustache and side whiskers who was upset about some papers and wanted the house for himself, whom Holzer later determined to be Thomas Whaley. There was a woman in the garden, the grandmother of the girl, and a few children in the nursery. Leek also spoke of a ghost who called himself Fedor and a man who said he had a bad fever that Holzer finally connected with Yankee Jim Robinson, after a little help from a San Diego local with an interesting spin—a spin that would change the way people would look at the Whaley House forever.

According to Holzer's book, *Ghosts:*

> My suspicions were confirmed when a letter written May 23, 1966 reached me. A Mrs. Carol DeJuhasz wanted me to know about a ghost at Whaley House... no, not Thomas Whaley or a twelve year old girl with long hair. Mrs. DeJuhasz was concerned with a historical play written by a friend of hers dealing with the unjust execution of a man who tried to steal a harbor boat in the 1800s

and was caught. Mrs. DeJuhasz merely thought he ought to be there, having been hanged in the backyard of the house.

In his book, Holzer first dismissed the possibility that the spirit was Robinson, then spends the next page justifying how it just may be the condemned man. DeJuhasz further claimed that Yankee Jim had fought a sabre duel when captured, received a critical head wound, and was tried without representation while delirious and "sick with fever." Leek had spoken of a man with a bad fever.

The Ballad of Yankee Jim was performed in June 1966 at the Whaley House through the Theatre Arts Guild of San Diego City College. A part-time guide, William Richardson, told Holzer in December 1966 that the performances seemed to increase the occurrences of ghostly phenomena. The actors felt the presence of Thomas and Anna, smelled cigar smoke, and experienced temperature changes. Richardson further believed that Yankee Jim had gotten a bad deal. He claimed Yankee Jim had only borrowed a boat, was unconscious for most of his trial,

Whaley House courtroom where the 1966 "Ballad of Yankee Jim" play was performed.

the judge was drunk, and, once sentenced to death, badly executed. Holzer concluded that Yankee Jim Robinson must be the presence detected by Leek and all references to Fedor and Calstrop were dropped.

Today, the Whaley House claims that the house is built on "the exact spot where Yankee Jim swung for his crimes." Since the paranormal investigations and play from the mid-1960s, the exact location of the gallows has been narrowed down even further to a spot under the archway between the parlor and the music room. People have reported feeling a constriction around their neck when they stand in this archway.

WHO WAS YANKEE JIM?

So just who was Yankee Jim? Was he a stocky man holding a whip or a man wandering around with a bad fever? The commonly told story of Yankee Jim Robinson is a sad one and often portrayed as an example of prairie justice in the American West. Yankee Jim Robinson was a drunk and trouble-maker in town who had spent some time working the gold fields up north. On August 13, 1852, he and two accomplices took a rowboat and tried to steal the *Plutus*, a large pilot boat or schooner out in the harbor. The owner of the *Plutus*, Captain James Keating, spotted them, ordered them back to shore, and even took a shot at them.

The men got away, but were eventually captured the next day. Yankee Jim was lassoed by a Mexican, hit on the head with a rusty sword, strapped onto a mule, and brought to town. Two days later, the men were tried for the crime of grand larceny. His two accomplices were given jail terms while Yankee Jim was sentenced to die by hanging.

After a thirty-day imprisonment, he was led to some scaffolding outside the main plaza to be executed. According to legend, because he was uncommonly tall and the rope not long enough, he died of strangulation instead of having his neck snapped as intended. It took him some time, according to some accounts, up to thirty minutes, to die before he was finally cut down and buried in El Campo Cemetery. It is also said that his executioner was none other than Philip Crosthwaite, Yankee Jim's godfather.

Yankee Jim Robinson's actual origin is unknown. Frances Bardacke, who wrote the 1966 play, *The Ballad of Yankee Jim*, came to the conclusion that he was from the East Coast, which would explain his nickname. But she was also quick to confess, in an article she wrote on researching the ill-fated criminal, that there were many "Yankee Jims" running around. Similar to other such criminal aliases as "Three-Fingered Jack", these names often appear throughout the history of the West. It's important to note that Bardacke considered her play a conception of historic personalities and a dramatic fiction—not a documentary.

But the story of Yankee Jim is a great example of events becoming more detailed over the years instead of more vague. There was a lengthy article on the capture of "the Notorious Yankee Jim" in the *San Diego Herald* dated August 27, 1852.

> By their own confession, and the statement of one corroborated that of another, they had come down from Stockton together, stealing and selling horses, and committing rascalities generally.

How long Yankee Jim was here before his capture is unclear, but what we do know is that he was a confessed troublemaker and horse thief. The people of early San Diego may have just been waiting for this renegade to cross the line so they could get rid of him forever. And remember, the men confessed to trying to steal the *Plutus*.

After his arrest, Yankee Jim's trial began only three days later. The "Records of the Court of Sessions, August 1852" provides the court minutes for the trial. The District Attorney was James W. Robinson, a very well-respected citizen, who is often confused with Yankee Jim. In fact, on the grave marker for Yankee Jim at El Campo Santo, it gives his name as "James W. Robinson," but there is no evidence of Yankee Jim's middle initial. If you ever see a picture purporting to be the Yankee Jim who was hanged, chances are it's a photo of James W. Robinson, a highly distinguished and prominent judge, attorney, and businessman.

The acting Sheriff was Joseph Reiner in the absence of Sheriff George Hooper. A Grand Jury was quickly assembled to present a Bill of Indictment against the men and Thomas Whaley was listed as part of that Grand Jury. However, he was not one of the twelve jurors who determined Yankee Jim's fate. Yankee Jim did manage to challenge several of the jurors presented and they were replaced, which contradicts the claim that he was unconscious during his trial. The man who owned the rowboat, which Yankee Jim took to get to the *Plutus,* was on the jury but not Captain Keating, the owner of the *Plutus* and an eyewitness to the crime. Yankee Jim was tried for attempting to steal the *Plutus*, which qualified as grand larceny. He was never charged for taking the small rowboat.

The jury deliberated for about thirty minutes; Robinson was found guilty and sentenced to be hanged thirty days later. His cohorts were each sentenced to a year imprisonment. The *San Diego Herald* wrote:

> There being no jail, and the Sheriff having no place to keep the prisoners, the citizens called a public meeting for the purpose of disposing of Robinson immediately, by hanging him to the nearest tree, but when the people got together at the Court House and talked the matter over coolly, wiser counsels prevailed.

In addition to the *San Diego Herald* article on the capture and trial of Yankee Jim, there were snippets about the arrest and conviction that appeared in the *Los Angeles Star*, the *Daily Alta California* and the *Sacramento Daily Union*. According to the August 28, 1852 edition of the *Los Angeles Star*,

> The charge upon which they were tried was for stealing a boat, but they are strongly suspected of horse-stealing and even murder.

The *Daily Alta* September 2, 1852 edition added:

> The prisoners have acknowledged that they were professional horse thieves.

No September 1852 editions of the *San Diego Herald* exist today nor the *Los Angeles Star* that might have covered the hanging. The *Daily Alta California* (September 23, 1852) and the *Sacramento Daily Union* (September 24, 1852) both briefly mention the hanging but few details. On the execution of Yankee Jim, the *Daily Alta* added:

> He made a long speech to the people and denied his guilt to the last moment. He also stated that nearly all the fires in San Francisco, Stockton, and Marysville were caused by incendiaries, out of revenge for the acts of the Vigilance Committee.

That's all that was written in 1852 at the time of Yankee Jim's execution. Thomas Whaley penned several letters during this time and even wrote his mother the day after the hanging, but none of them mention the incident or Yankee Jim at all. He does write, however, that he is very busy with his business, "engaged night and day at least 18 hours out of the 24." There is simply no evidence that Whaley was present at the hanging of Yankee Jim, nor is a location for the hanging given.

The next article on the demise of Yankee Jim doesn't appear until the *San Diego Union* October 4, 1873 edition, twenty-one years after the event and when most of the principals at the trial were deceased. The article, entitled "How the Pioneers Disposed of Offensive People" claims that the charge was stealing a rowboat which was later discovered and belonged to two of the men on the jury. There's no mention of the pilot boat, the *Plutus*, or Captain Keating. The article mentions that the gallows "consisted of two beams planted in the ground with a heavy bar across the top. It was located in Old Town, on the spot where Whaley's brick house now stands." It also describes in detail the death of Yankee Jim:

> He swung back and forth like a pendulum until he strangled to death. And thus ended the career of the dreaded desperado Yankee Jim.

Yankee Jim next appeared in an article in the *San Diego Union* dated February 25, 1894, nearly forty-two years after Yankee Jim's death and strangely gives even more details about the origins of Yankee Jim, such as where he was born, his physical features, what he liked to drink, and his daring robberies. It's a very colorful tale of a bad man with a lengthy criminal past who got convicted of stealing an old whale boat. The account of the hanging was provided by old settlers who remembered a rude scaffold erected around the hill south of Old Town. Crosthwaite supervised the hanging, but when asked if he had anything to say, Yankee Jim replied, "Nothing." He was hanged, cut down, and buried in a nearby grave.

So was Yankee Jim hanged on Whaley property? Quite possibly, but we'll never know for sure. Over the early years, Thomas Whaley purchased up to twelve acres of land all over Old Town area on several lots. No newspaper from 1852 mentions the place of execution. The 1873 article states that the gallows were "on the spot where Whaley's brick house now stands," while the 1894 edition says that the scaffold was erected "around the hill south of Old Town." June Reading claimed that Yankee Jim was hanged by a tree that Thomas later cut down and built a house on its roots—which is exactly where the archway is today. But there is absolutely no mention of the location of the gallows where Yankee Jim was hanged until twenty-one years had passed. I've seen pictures and drawings of Old Town in the 1850s and there aren't any trees around. It was flat and desolate. From other historic records, we know that people were executed in the main plaza and sometimes near the El Campo Cemetery. The truth is, we simply don't know.

Did Thomas Whaley tell his children that the house was built on the execution grounds and that Yankee Jim haunted the family home? We have no proof of that, either. It doesn't appear in his personal letters, only through the words of June Reading, recounting Corrine's words. It's a good time to mention that Reading probably never met Corrine Whaley, for Corrine moved into a rest home in 1952, and Reading didn't even see the house for the first time until the following year.

In Corrine Whaley's *California's Oldest Town*, a compilation of childhood memories which Reading edited and published in 1980, there is no mention of the home being built on the old execution grounds or Yankee Jim, but does say that she used to tell neighboring Mexican children that her house was haunted by "ghosts with big eyes." In June Reading's own book, *The Thomas Whaley House,* published by the Historical Shrine Foundation in 1960, there is also no mention of the house being built where Yankee Jim met his demise, let alone under the exact location of the interior archway.

Benjamin Radford, famed paranormal investigator and skeptic, has stated that when dealing with historical ghost stories, they should become more muddled

Representation of grave of Yankee Jim Robinson. Real site of grave is unknown.

with age, not include more details, like the 1894 article. Almost everyone who was present at the trial of Yankee Jim was either long dead or near death by this time, so why more details? There are no other newspaper articles. I could find no letters, especially in those of Thomas Whaley, who according to legend and told today by the Whaley House staff, attended the hanging. I have looked at all of his available letters of the time period surrounding the execution of Yankee Jim, and there is simply no mention of it.

The 1894 article does note that the body hanged there for thirty minutes before Dr. Painter, the physician that was assigned to the task, checked Yankee Jim's heart to confirm that he was dead before being cut down. There is no mention that it took him thirty minutes to die. In fact, the article says "death soon relieved his suffering"—so much for kicking and convulsing as legend states.

Why did they wait 30 minutes? It was probably standard procedure. I'm sure plenty of bodies were left on display for a bit before cutting them down and checking for a pulse as a formality. The mixing of the two newspaper articles as well as a healthy dose of urban legend form the Yankee Jim story that we know today. The word "strangulation" and the given time span of thirty minutes makes it seem that Yankee Jim danced from the rope like a wicked marionette, and that simply isn't true.

ANOTHER HORSE THIEF

No journey to the famous Whaley House is complete without a stop by the El Campo Santo, the local cemetery. Once you walk through the main gate, you will stumble across...the grave of Yankee Jim. On the headstone is the story I mentioned at the beginning of the chapter, in all its highly questionable glory. It even states that Crosthwaite, the under-sheriff at the time, was Jim's godfather as well as his executioner. Maybe. But why would a county clerk, sheriff, and Master of the first Masonic Lodge in San Diego become the godfather of a confessed horse thief from Stockton?

I believe the confusion stems from the story of another alleged horse thief, William Marshall, who was convicted of high treason and immediately hanged in San Diego nine months before Yankee Jim decided to take a boat out for a ride. There are a lot of similarities between this story and the legend of Yankee Jim. By his own confession, William Marshall came to San Diego in 1846, and ran a store out in Agua Caliente (Warner Springs), most likely for Juan Jose Warner, owner of the rancho. General Stephen Watts Kearny passed through Warner's Ranch, spoke with Marshall, and four days later fought with the Californios at the Battle of San Pasqual.

Until statehood was granted in September 1850, California was under military rule. In 1847, Warner accused Marshall of stealing some mules, horses, and other items, but Marshall was found innocent and the matter dropped. Marshall continued to work at Agua Caliente, owned property, and was among the first taxpayers of San Diego County.

Indians were taxed as well and this created a deep resentment. Rumors of an impending Indian attack grew, largely instigated by Antonio Garra, the chief of Agua Caliente, who was trying to rally the neighboring tribes into attacking the Americans.

At the last minute, Garra claimed he was ill and stayed behind. The Cahuillas near Warner's Ranch and the Cupeño of Agua Caliente attacked Agua Caliente on November 21, 1851, and killed four Americans. Marshall, who lived there with his Indian wife and infant son, later confessed that he was forewarned of the attack, but threatened with death if he alerted the Americans. The next day, Warner's Ranch was attacked by Indians, but Warner escaped in the gunfire. His home and store were ransacked and burned, his livestock driven off. The warring Indians, with Marshall in tow, gathered in Coyote Canyon north of Borrego Valley. Warner, meanwhile, made it to San Diego; martial law was declared and a group of men called Fitzgerald's Volunteers was assembled to go after the Indians.

Garra was still trying to unify the Indian tribes for full-scale war when he was betrayed, captured, and turned over to a volunteer company from Los Angeles. Garra's son and four others were executed in Los Angeles but Garra was taken down to San Diego. Marshall was caught in Santa Ysabel and brought to San Diego where he was considered an active participant in the revolt, despite his protestations and corroborating testimony. On December 12, 1851, although he was found not guilty of being an accessory to robbery and murder, Marshall was found guilty of high treason and sentenced to be hanged.

The next morning, a gallows was constructed near the Catholic burying grounds and graves dug. According to *Record Book of Mission San Diego de Alcala—Book II*, Marshall was baptized that morning by Father Holbein with Philip Crosthwaite standing as his godfather. Years later, the 1860 U.S. Census would show that Manuel Marshall, a 9-year old Indian boy, was living in the Crosthwaite household.

The *San Diego Herald* dated December 18, 1851 described Marshall's execution in detail, his last words asking for forgiveness and claims of innocence. The fall did not dislocate his neck, Marshall struggled considerably and death took about forty-five minutes.

Antonio Garra got his day in court and was found guilty of robbery, treason, and murder by a militia court on January 17, 1852, and sentenced to death by firing squad. On that same day, Garra was marched from his cell to a freshly dug grave in El Campo Santo. He was reportedly calm and when asked if he had anything to confess, answered:

Gentlemen, I ask your pardon for all my offenses, and expect yours in return.

He was blindfolded, told to kneel, and the order to fire was given. According to his letters, Thomas Whaley, as a member of Fitzgerald's Volunteers, was "one of the twelve men who were ordered to execute the sentence."

So here we have detailed documentation of the execution of Antonio Garra, a man who taunted his firing squad, and was shot by Thomas Whaley, near his house at El Campo Santo. Yet we are told that Whaley instead believed that his house was haunted by a boat thief from Stockton whom he never wrote about, with no evidence that he ever interacted with, nor as to the location of the gallows. There are too many similarities, as well, between the hanging of William Marshall and the notorious legend of Yankee Jim Robinson to ignore. There was only ten months separating the two hangings and since the most detailed accounts didn't come until twenty-one and forty-two years after the hanging, it follows logic that old timers might have confused the two.

ANNA BELLE WASHBURN

Another famous haunt attached to the Whaley House is that of Anna Belle Washburn, the young girl who Leek associated with the house during her 1965 visit. To the credit of the Whaley House official website, they dismiss the story as false, lacking in physical evidence, and "probably made up by a former employee."

According to the legend, Anna Belle, or Carrie Washburn (depending on who you ask) was a neighbor of the Whaley's, and while playing in the backyard, managed to catch her neck on the clothes line and her trachea was crushed. In some stories, Thomas found the young girl and placed her on the kitchen table where she expired and that is why the Whaley kitchen is haunted by the ghost of a little girl that plays with the items found there. All you have to do is *Google* it and the story appears over and over again.

When I ran my own tour, I heard that story so many times, in so many ways, it makes my head spin just thinking about it. Variations from she was walking along a wall surrounding the property and fell on the line which crushed her throat to (my personal favorite) that she ran down the hill and the rope decapitated her. Really? She would have had to run like a cheetah and the clothesline would had to have been made of cheese-wire. My heart broke when a guest on my tour once recounted the story and said she heard it from her daughter. Her daughter was told the story from her school teacher on a field trip in Old Town—a field trip that was designed to teach local kids early San Diego history, not keep them awake at night with urban myth. There isn't really a thing about the story that's true. It started as an offshoot from the Hans Holzer/ Sybil Leek investigations of the house in the 1960s, as noted in the *San Diego Union* July 7, 1968:

Holzer: "Did anything unusual transpire?"

Leek: "I was standing in the entrance hall, looking at the postcards when I felt I just had to go to the kitchen, but I didn't go there first, but went halfway up the stairs, and a child came down the stairs into the kitchen and I followed her."

Holzer: "A child?"

Leek: "It was a long-haired child. She was very quick, you know, in a longish dress. She went to the table in this room and I went to the chair. That's all I remember."

Later:

Leek: This room where you found me sitting. I found myself drawn to it. The impressions are very strong here. Especially, that child... What's her name? Anna...Bell... She died very suddenly with something, when she was 13... chest...

From that brief moment spawned legend. I was always fascinated by the story and investigating it was a pleasure. There are plenty of books about the Whaley House ghosts and almost all of them cover the Washburn story. Robert Wlodarski in his books, *The Haunted Whaley House I* and *II*, covered the story in-depth from a mystery monger's point of view. John Lamb's *Spectral San Diego* also covers the story, but simply took hearsay from June Reading and others along with a trip down to the San Diego History Center's archives, coming back with what most do: urban myth accepted as truth.

When I first tackled the story, I checked for any newspaper accounts of a young girl dying at the Whaley House or in such a manner in Old Town. Finding nothing, I searched census records for a family named Washburn during the years the Whaleys lived in the house. Again, I drew a blank. Even reading through Thomas' letters failed to turn up any evidence that this tragedy occurred at his house. There is just no historic documentation of such an event that I could find.

So I went to the local cemeteries. Mt. Hope was the first mega cemetery in San Diego and that's where most of the bodies at the time were laid to rest. I perused its directory and came across A.B. Washburn. I was ecstatic to say the least. I parked my car near the Whaley plots and walked the beautiful cemetery, enjoying the crisp morning air. I found what I was looking for on accident. I was originally looking for Kate Morgan, the young woman who is said to haunt the Hotel del Coronado and between her and the Whaley plot was the gravestone for Anna B. Washburn. An infant of only three months, this Anna died in 1892, many years after the Whaleys moved from Old Town and, as a baby, hardly fits the candidacy for the story.

Anna B. Washburn grave, Mt. Hope Cemetery.

I honestly believe that the name came from Sybil Leek when she originally came to San Diego for the Whaley House investigations. She may have attempted a "hot" read and went to Mt. Hope before the actual investigation started to gather as much information about the family as she could beforehand. Anna's tombstone isn't that far away from the Whaley's and she may have just plucked the name to make the story more plausible, though this has not been documented. Also, in Reading's 1960 book, *The Thomas Whaley House*, there is mention of a small outer adobe building that was whitewashed and once stood near the Whaley House. It was referred to as the Washburn house, although it was never a residence.

MARION LOUISE REYNOLDS

The sad part about the Anna Belle Washburn story is that it is sometimes interwoven with a real family tragedy. Marion Louise Reynolds, age two, died of accidental poisoning just three weeks before her third birthday. She was the great granddaughter of Thomas Whaley. According to the *San Diego Union,* dated August 6, 1912, Reynolds discovered ant poison, which was sugar mixed with arsenic, in an abandoned home where she was playing with her friends. She died August 4, 1912 at 12 p.m., in the city of Oceanside, approximately forty-five miles north of San Diego, and was buried in Los Angeles.

Marion Reynolds, second from left, at her home in Oceanside.

So how did the story of Marion Louise Reynolds get tied into the mythos of the Whaley House? Many times I have heard about the ghost of a little girl who haunts the dining room/kitchen area of the Whaley House. *TAPS Paramagazine* ran an article from an investigator visiting the home in 2011 and included Marion as one of the possible ghosts there. Somewhere along the line, people attempted to explain the paranormal activity of the museum or simply wished to add spice to the mystery, dug into the family history, and breathed new life into her by changing the story around here and there to make it fit their purposes.

But Marion consumed poison in an abandoned house and died in Oceanside. In 1912, the Whaley House had recently been restored by Francis Whaley and was occupied by the remaining Whaley family. The Whaley House has not corrected these exaggerations. Quite the opposite. On a recent visit to the Whaley House gift shop, I stumbled across a book on the ghost stories associated to the famous haunt and it stated that a girl died in the kitchen from accidental poisoning. In this book though, they give her age as 12 or 13, thus tying in the Holzer/ Leek séance. I would like to remove Marion Reynolds from the long list of specters possessing this abode, but then again, what's an extra body or two in America's Most Haunted?

THE NINTH STEP

One of the most mind-boggling ghost stories I have encountered about the Whaley House is that of the ninth step. According to legend, the staircase carries some paranormal energy associated with Anna Whaley. The story stems from the time when the County rented out the old granary room for a courthouse and three rooms upstairs for storage. This is also at the time when New Town San Diego was developing and Old Town was slowly fading away. The County built a new courthouse in the New Town area early, and, in essence, broke its lease with Whaley a couple of months early.

In the popular telling of the story, residents of Old Town refused to give up the court records and a form of martial law was instilled to protect the records from being transferred over without the back rent being paid to Whaley. Things eventually quieted down and Thomas had to go to San Francisco on business, leaving Anna and the children alone. While he was gone, armed men broke into the house, terrorized the family, and held Anna and the children hostage at gunpoint on the staircase. To this day, guests and employees feel an unusual cold spot around the ninth step of the house.

I have also heard stories of guests being pushed down the stairs by unseen hands. Some say that Thomas himself haunts the Whaley House in anger over the supposed hostilities.

How much of the story about the ninth step is true? Unfortunately, not very much. There are many holes in the story about the incident surrounding the court records and the transfer to New Town in April 1871. The power transfer was a lot more amicable than legend would have you believe. Thomas Whaley himself even purchased property in the New Town area, moved his business there in 1870, and later built a home in New Town after the suicide of his daughter.

Whaley house (in)famous stairwell.

Was the house ever broken into and Anna held at gunpoint, as the legend states time and again? The best historic evidence is in Thomas Whaley's own personal papers that you can read online at the Whaley House website. The papers themselves are incredibly difficult to read, some are unintelligible and the ink is so faded that attempting to decipher them is nearly impossible. Luckily though, the time of the court papers being transferred was covered. The letters completely contradict the theory that Thomas was out of town as he corresponded frequently with his daughter in San Francisco during March-May 1871, mostly relaying the demise of Old Town.

Did masked gunmen break in the windows to get into the house? In a June 28, 1871 letter to the County, Thomas does mention "lights of glass broken out during the occupancy of the premises" and asked that they be replaced as per the terms of the lease. He also asks that "all county property be removed from the premises and that the keys be delivered to me." Legend also states that Thomas was never paid for the back rent, but the reality is that he was later fully compensated by the County.

In fact, in none of the letters could I find evidence that the house was broken into. His letters to the County throughout 1871 regarding the matter were quite professional and, of course, there is no mention of Anna and the children being held hostage. That's because it probably never happened. There is no historic documentation that a confrontation ever took place. To the contrary, according to newspaper articles that appeared in the *San Diego Bulletin* and the *San Diego Union* on April 4, 1871, it was "a peaceful transition—all the archives of San Diego County passed quietly and honorably from the oldest city in California to its young but lusty neighbor. It was inevitable."

There's also debate as to whether or not Thomas and his family were even living in the house at the time of the transfer. Three rooms upstairs and the courthouse were being rented out by the County and another business was downstairs, so the idea that the Whaley family of seven was living alongside them in the small house is dubious. Thomas' request that the keys be returned to him and reference to the premises being left in a good state doesn't sound like he was sleeping in the next room.

The best part about tackling classic ghost stories is that they have a tendency to snowball. You follow one trail of evidence and it turns into another trail and so forth. I find it amazing how much history is hidden if it doesn't support the image that parties wish to convey. For example, I have found many times on the Internet and in books that cover the Whaley House that the Whaley family lived in the house from its construction in 1856 to the time they moved to New Town in November 1885.

After it was constructed, Thomas lived in the house for a year before he decided to pack up the family under the invitation of an old friend and business partner Major George H. Ringgold, and move back to San Francisco. He left all his business dealing to Frank Ames, a business partner and Wells Fargo agent, including the renting out of the house. The Whaley family did not return to San Diego until the summer of 1868—ten years later.

In their absence, several families rented out the house, and when the Whaley's returned to San Diego, they were forced to live elsewhere in Old Town while repairs were made to the house, for Thomas' letters indicate that the house was in a sad state. I found an ad in the newspaper from October 24, 1868 by Thomas attempting to sell or lease the house. He described it in great detail and offered to let it go "as is" or fix it up for "any responsible party desiring to take a lease." One of the interesting things I found reading Thomas Whaley's personal letters is that he never referred to the house as "our house." Many times he simply refers to it as "the brick building."

In December of 1868, the Tanner Troupe, a small acting group, rented out the front upstairs bedroom and opened a theatre that seated approximately 150 people. Tanner himself died only 17 days after the theatre opening—a very small time in history for the Whaley House, yet if you visit there today, you will see a full reproduction of the theatre. SOHO touts the Tanner Troupe as being the first theatre in San Diego, but the first recorded theatrical performances were in 1858 at the San Diego Mission. That same year, soldiers produced six plays at the Franklin House in Old Town.

In June, 1869, I found a newspaper article stating that the Union Republic party of San Diego used the building for meetings to nominate party members. It stated that they rented out a "suite of rooms in the 2nd story of the brick building belonging to Thomas Whaley of Old Town." Then, in August, 1869, the County of San Diego leased out three rooms upstairs and the granary for use as a courthouse. In February 1870, a Rev. I.H. Cox was holding Sunday services at 11 a.m. and 7 p.m. at "Whaley's brick building." The large room has been used as a billiard room, a kindergarten, a dairy, a courtroom, Sunday school, store, post office, and residence, but never as a morgue or jail, as some websites have claimed. Still, this doesn't exactly seem like the family home for Thomas and his wife along with five kids. There are only four rooms upstairs and one bedroom downstairs with a parlor and small living room. With the courthouse leasing three rooms upstairs, where did the family go?

When you visit the Whaley House today, you see a family home with a courthouse and a small general store. The rest of the house is the family's, but in truth, it is highly doubtful that the house ever looked like what you see today. It was used for commercial purposes for so many years that's it's difficult to visualize it as a family home. The census shows that the Whaley's lived in San Diego and I saw envelopes that were addressed to them. Sadly, though, it just listed "Thomas Whaley, San Diego." The town was so small, no physical address was necessary. I have also found evidence that for some time they rented out several homes in the Old Town area including the Burkhardt House and Gila House.

Whaley House theatre recreation, which was in operation only seventeen days.

VIOLENCE AT A HUSBAND'S HAND

There is one last ghost story of a woman who was gutted by her jealous husband, perhaps in reference to the distraught woman psychically seen by Kay Sterner in 1962 with a straight-edge razor in her hand. In a second visit by the California Parapsychology Foundation a few months later, when no evidence was recorded, it was said:

> One of our sensitives, a woman, claimed she saw a woman with a knife wound in the stomach. According to a foundation spokesperson, a man and wife who rented a room at the house in the early 1900s had a violent quarrel and the man stabbed his wife in the stomach.

Sometimes this story is associated with the Tanner Troupe's occupation of the house back in 1868, but it's unlikely such an event ever occurred with Thomas in town. Needless to say, there is no historic documentation that such a crime ever took place at the Whaley House. In fact, when Francis Whaley moved back to the house in 1909, it was in complete disrepair, the windows boarded up, which is evidenced in photos.

AN AUTHOR PERSPECTIVE

It's interesting to note that although it is well documented that several members of the Whaley family did expire in the house—infant Thomas of scarlet fever, Violet by suicide, 81-year-old Anna, and Francis at age 60—the four main ghosts thought to inhabit the Whaley House only includes one of them (Anna).

It is so easy for stories over the years to become more and more convoluted. Not for one minute do I believe that the Whaley House isn't haunted, for there are far too many instances of people experiencing things for me to sum them up as mass hysteria. In my employment there, even I have had an experience which I cannot explain. It was in the summer and I was working there as a docent whose job was to let in the evening "ghost tour" and watch over the house as they stumbled around in hopes of experiencing something from the Other Side.

The tour hadn't arrived yet and my coworker had gone down the street to fetch some coffee. The house was under some restoration at the time and the downstairs hallway light wasn't functioning. I usually read to pass the time between tours and so settled in the hallway. Due to the lack of light, I was forced to position my chair in the doorway between the parlor and the hallway, using the parlor's light to read. I was several pages in when I felt suddenly very cold.

Remember, it was summer and I was dressed in stuffy Victorian clothing, but I was definitely chilled. I became more and more distressed at the thought that I felt someone behind me as if they were reading over my shoulder. I quietly closed the book and then leapt up and turned around to face...nothing. My imagination or a brush with the paranormal? I myself cannot explain the intense cold on that hot summer's evening, but the unexplained doesn't necessarily mean unexplainable. Nobody wants the answer to that riddle more than I.

VISITOR INFORMATION

Whaley House Museum
2476 San Diego Avenue, San Diego, CA 92110
(619) 297-7511
http://whaleyhouse.org

CHAPTER FOUR

NEW TOWN, NEW GHOST

HORTON GRAND HOTEL

Roger A. Whitaker, gambler and pimp, was living in the Stingaree district (the former red-light district), and was caught one night cheating at cards. That cheating earned him a bullet in the gut, though he managed to flee the scene of the shooting. Stumbling back to his hotel room, he crawled into the armoire, unsure if his wounds were fatal. There he cowered in fear, until his assassin tracked him down by a trail of blood back to his hotel, and finished the job. The sound of a single shot rang through the hotel and Roger passed on to the Other Side.

Today, at the Horton Grand Hotel, it seems Roger is still up to his old tricks. Guests have made claims such as being kept up all night with the sounds of a poker game that they cannot locate and lights being turned off and on. Not just cold spots, but extreme heat, has been recorded in one room, even though the hotel staff can find nothing wrong with the thermostat. I have even read a story about a deck of cards being laid out and finding a hand dealt out upon the return of the nonspectral guests. Room 309 of this historic hotel is the permanent residence of Roger A. Whittaker.

Or is it?

As San Diego expanded first into an American town, and then a true Victorian town, industrious men such as Alonzo Horton were attracted to this sleepy hamlet. Horton had worked as a river boat captain and merchant, and founded

Horton Grand Hotel.

a town in Wisconsin called "Hortonville." He was lured to Northern California by the gold fields, but found success as a merchant/supplier and capitalized during San Francisco's booming population. After hearing about San Diego's climate, ample space, and proposed railroad, he made his way down to San Diego like many others in 1867. After surveying the current layout of the town, he had the vision of San Diego not only as a small port town, but as a bustling harbor with warehouses and docks.

Horton purchased 960 acres of marshland at twenty-seven and a half cents an acre. He financed a port to be built that would utilize the larger bay, and merchants, as well as others, came to buy these new coastal tracts of land. In 1885, the Santa Fe Train Depot was built to accommodate the arrival of the California

Southern Railroad, which brought even more people from *back east*. With the gold boom in the nearby town of Julian, the railroad and the new waterfront, New Town San Diego became a bustling seaport. But busy seaports draw all kinds of people, and not all of them good.

Brothels, opium dens, and press gangs began to spring up and were all too common in New Town by the beginning of the 1880s. A goodly portion of Horton's new design became a red-light district, affectionately known as the "Stingaree." Stingaree is sailor's slang for a stingray. It was said that you were more likely to be "stung" in the Stingaree district than in the nearby ray-infested waters themselves. Bars with such colorful names as the Seven Buckets of Blood, Green Light, and Old Tub of Blood littered the district and usually operated as a front for all kinds of vices.

The practice of shanghaiing was in full swing here. The idea of getting drunk and waking up on a ship miles out to sea as a member of a crew you didn't sign up for would make a man want to drink lightly, you'd think, but it usually didn't. It was also not unheard of to get sailors drunk or high so that they would miss reporting back to duty. Once the allotted waiting time was up and the sailor was declared AWOL, the still-woozy sailor would be duly returned and the reward collected by a "concerned citizen."

The official boundaries of the red-light district were always in contest, but the Health Department at the time laid it out as First to Fifth, and Market to K. This area was pretty much a free-for-all for all sorts of debauchery. Most of what took place in this area was illegal, but grafts and payoffs were common to the local police in fledgling New Town. Nearly 100 brothels were in business at the time; it was confined to a certain area and business was good.

The Stingaree stayed that way until it finally buckled under political pressure and was shut down in 1912. Plans were already being laid out for the Panama-California Exposition, scheduled to take place in 1915, and San Diego couldn't very well be a cosmopolitan city with such an unsavory reputation. With so many brothels in operation, such as Ida Bailey's Canary Cottage, something had to be done to bring things to order.

On November 11, 1912, a raid was staged and all types of undesirables poured out into the streets when the police showed up in force to shut the district down. Arrested that night were 138 prostitutes—136 of them agreed to leave the city (though most bought round-trip train tickets to Los Angeles), while 2 agreed to be reformed. The Stingaree was finally out of business in preparation for the Exposition. But unfortunately, the illegal activities returned and merely spread throughout the county.

That part of downtown though never truly recovered. I remember, as a young man, I was not allowed to venture down there for anything. It never regained its popularity until the Gaslamp Quarter restoration of the 1980s. Today, it's a string of upscale shops, trendy restaurants, and nightclubs, the original brick and ornate wood exteriors a staple for this nighttime draw. The downtown area is once more a popular gathering place.

At the southernmost end of the new Gaslamp Quarter is an architectural beauty. Originally three separate hotels, the Horton Grand Hotel now serves as a reminder of days gone by. Two of the hotels, the main part that lines Island Avenue from Fourth to Fifth Streets, were originally from different parts of town. The Grand Horton, which once stood where the Westfield Horton Plaza shopping center is today, was a replica of the Innsbruck Hotel in Vienna, Austria, and commissioned by a wealthy German immigrant.

The other hotel, which was once located on Market Street, was known as the Brooklyn. It was a much simpler hotel that housed many gamblers and other interesting characters. One of their most famous long-term guests was none other than Wyatt Earp, who lived in San Diego from 1885 to possibly 1896. Later, the bottom floor of the Brooklyn was home to the Kahle Saddlery, where fine saddles and other horse trappings were made for Tom Mix, Roy Rogers, and other famous Hollywood cowboys. Sunshine, a paper mache horse, is an artifact from the shop and still resides in the lobby of the Horton Grand Hotel today.

These two hotels were slated for destruction in the 1970s and were bought by the City of San Diego for $1 a piece. The redwood interiors of the hotels were traded for labor to dismantle and move the new structures to its current home. Over 10,000 pieces were stored in a warehouse, each individually numbered, and when the land became available for redevelopment, they were reassembled brick-by-brick at the new location. The atrium that joins the two hotels was added when the Horton Grand Hotel opened for business in May 1986.

The third hotel is behind the Brooklyn portion of the hotel and was originally the Anita and Regal Hotel. This hotel was one of the stops of the "Great Raid" of 1912. It was reopened in 1990, offers additional suites, and connects to the Horton Grand via a sky bridge.

Visitors from all over stay at this boutique hotel for many different reasons—the high tea served on the weekends, its ideal location, the Victorian charm that adorns its walls and rooms. But many check into one room for a very specific reason: ghosts. I like to walk the lobby and halls of the Horton Grand Hotel. It seems so easy to close my eyes and open them again to over a hundred years ago, when Wyatt Earp walked down these halls with one Roger A. Whitaker. That is, of course, if Roger ever existed.

ROGER A WHITAKER

Working in the history field for many years, I learned that one good asset that any paranormal investigator should have is research and I came up with some very interesting results. One, there is no tangible evidence of the actual existence of Roger A. Whitaker, let alone a murder. No police reports. No coroner's inquest. No announcements in the newspaper at the time. We couldn't even locate him in any census or directory. Could he have existed? Perhaps, but not on paper, which even in those days was a pretty difficult thing to do—especially if you were gunned down in a public place. Someone knew you or did business with you, and records were kept.

The earliest reference to Roger Whitaker that I could find was a *San Diego Union Tribune* article dated November 23, 1987, eighteen months after the Horton Grand Hotel opened for business. I am unable to locate any other reference to Roger A. Whitaker prior to 1987.

The first person to report strange happenings in Room 209 was a chambermaid at the Horton Grand named Martha Mays. She reported not being able to get into the room because the deadbolt was locked from the inside. The armoire door opened and closed on its own accord. The light turned itself back on.

A long list of happenings prompted the hotel management to conduct an investigation of the room and hire a local psychic, Shelley Deegan, to discover where the spirit came from. Deegan brought another psychic, Jacqueline Williams, with her along with a flowering plant and some purified water. The two spent the night in Room 309 at the hotel's request with television crews and reporters in tow. Although the ghost remained in hiding while the news crews were present, after they left, the ghost is said to have communicated telepathically with the psychics.

According to Deegan, Roger told her his full name, his occupation as a pimp and gambler, and that he was 37 years old when gunned down by a gambling associate. When Roger was asked who was President the year he died, Roger telepathically told them Grover Cleveland (who was president from 1885 to 1889 and 1893 to 1897). Deegan said that Roger also mentioned the year 1846.

I looked up Deegan and she's still in business today. According to her website, she's a rent-a-psychic. She and her staff are hired for company parties, for giving Tarot card readings, astrology, and palmistry. One of her taglines is "Completely Upbeat." I contacted the psychic several times for confirmation, but did not receive a reply.

The encounter with the Other Side that this psychic and her companion experienced was charming and, if anything, alarming to anyone who might want to spend the night in a haunted hotel room. It's curious though how we can know so much about a spirit in its state of death, yet we can find absolutely nothing about him in life to confirm these kinds of impressions. She claimed that while Roger was a little intense, he was friendly and harmless. I have studied a lot about the Stingaree and red-light districts in general in the United States and "friendly and harmless" are usually not the adjectives I associate with gamblers, dudes, and pimps.

Of all the psychic's claims, one item is important to note. She said that Roger never lived at the hotel at all and was not killed in the armoire that sits in Room 309, but simply *feels* comfortable there. Somehow, this simple fact is overlooked by almost all other sources I found that relate this tale. Gail White's *Haunted San Diego* as well as Robert Wlodarski's *California Ghosts* both fail to mention this. They relate the story of the ghostly gambler as though he resided in the hotel the entire time which, remember, is actually three separate hotels that were scattered in different parts of town. In fact, every story we have about Roger originally came from two 1987 newspaper articles. There is no mention or evidence of him anywhere prior to November 1987.

There is another version of the story that I found in print in a book on "ghostly legends" in which Roger was killed by his fiancé's father or his father-in-law in the 1840s in the vicinity of where the hotel now stands. That story, most likely an attempt to tie into Deegan's account that Roger mentioned 1846, is actually very easy to dismiss. During that time, when the shooting allegedly took place, the land that makes up what is now downtown San Diego, was Mission Rancho San Diego, Mexico. In fact, all of California didn't become a United States holding until 1848, eventually joining the Union in 1850. Now that is not to say that there were not any non-Hispanic people there at the time; there were. But with a non-Indian population of 650 in 1850 for all of San Diego County, that drastically cuts down the possibility of one Roger A. Whitaker, gambler and pimp.

Also, the land that was there at the time was actually a swamp and didn't become habitable until much later. If Roger was indeed shot and moved there, you would have to travel quite the distance of an inhospitable swamp just to dump a body. Where does this story come from? No one truly knows. Urban legend—it's the bane of any serious paranormal investigation.

When I originally ran my tours in San Diego, I approached the hotel and asked if my guests could come inside. They denied me, but were happy to allow me to talk about their famous ghost story from the sidewalk. Fair enough. Later, when I began to dig into the stories and theories for an article I was writing for a local magazine about haunted sites, I found that the Horton Grand Hotel only had a photocopy of the *Union Tribune* article and little other ghostly data for me that would confirm any part of the story.

Could Room 309 of the Horton Grand Hotel be haunted? Perhaps there is something there trying to reach out from the beyond. In each room of the Horton Grand, there is a diary for guests to record their stay. Room 309's diary reads like a bad horror novel. I have stayed several times in the room and each time there was a new diary there for people to write their experiences. There may be true experiences within those diaries, but they are lost when surrounded by others that seem less than genuine.

OTHER STORIES

There are other stories as well surrounding the hotel. I have heard and read that the hotel may also be haunted by the ghost of Ida Bailey, the well-known Madame in the Stingaree district. One story is that the hotel was built on what used to be her Bordello, the famous Canary Cottage. Close, but no cigar. The Cottage was actually across the street with a very unusual entrance that you had to enter through to get to it.

During the "Great Raid" of 1912, it is told by local legend only and a few tour guides, that when the cops busted down the alley toward Ida's house of ill repute, the mayor and police chief were spotted hopping the fence along with the rest of the clients. That doesn't seem plausible, though, because they would have had foreknowledge of the raid. Seems politics *does* make strange bedfellows.

Perhaps Ida does haunt the hotel due to its proximity to her old place of business. Or maybe she calls the place home because the hotel honors her so. The restaurant at the Horton Grand is named after the famous Madame and there is a portrait of her at the entrance.

According to the 1987 *Tribune* articles, there were also reports by the hotel guests of several other spirits that haunt the historic hotel, including a man dressed in western garb and a young boy. The staff has even come to name them, perhaps a way of comforting themselves when they come across something from the Beyond.

In the *San Diego Union*, dated November 25, 1987, giving the account of the psychic's overnight adventure, there's one last interesting note. After the initial article two days before, the hotel switchboard was flooded with calls from people who wanted to know more about the ghosts and to make reservations. According to the hotel marketing director:

> That room is booked from now (1987) until 1990.

Great job, Roger! A ghost is born.

VISITOR INFORMATION

Horton Grand Hotel
311 Island Ave, San Diego, CA 92101
(619) 544-1886
www.hortongrand.com

THE MARIN BUILDING

When someone asks me what my favorite haunt is down in the Gaslamp Quarter, it's simple: the Marin Building. Located right down the street from the Horton Grand Hotel on Fifth Avenue, this slice of Victorian Gothic brick built in 1888 was originally the Marin Hotel and carries its own dark past. Most passersby don't even know it's there, clouded in the neon and fast foot traffic of weekend Gaslamp revelers.

EDWARD W. TEBBUTT

I could so easily go into the history of what makes this canary yellow building special, but I think I would rather open with *The San Diego Union* dated June 3, 1894:

> Yesterday morning at 7 o'clock, when Ed Pigeon, employed by Gray and Co., furniture dealers at 552 Fifth Street, went to the store to open up, he found E.W. Tebbutt, a member of the firm, lying in the doorway of the back room, dead, with a pistol in his right hand and a hole in the top of his head.

The article went on to the specifics of the suicide, but most of the valuable information was gathered from the Coroner's Inquest dated June 3, 1894. Tebbutt did not seem to be a man who was looking for a way out. According to coworkers and friends, he was quiet, but most attributed it to the fact that he was a widower getting up there in the years and that he recently suffered from what we would call today as sun stroke. He took a nasty fall when he collapsed and bore a limp from a back injury since the malady struck him. Giving no sign of being suicidal, Pigeon must have been very surprised to come to work to see Tebbutt's life extinguished in such a violent manner.

According to the inquest, the gun was placed in his mouth and exited the crown of his head with such force that it blew an eye out of its socket. The bullet lodged into the opposite wall, approximately fifteen feet away and a splattering of brain and bone left his skull and followed the same trajectory as the bullet.

Edward W. Tebbutt, born in England in 1830, worked for John N. Young since 1870 and worked at the Gray and Co. Furniture store since 1883. The furniture company was well known in New Town as casket and coffin manufacturers of excellent reputation with a coroner to perform autopsies, as well as embalming down in the basement. For many years, Tebbutt lived in an apartment room at the back of the store and lived his life, hiding his secret pain till he could bear it no more.

Marin Building.

On a more modern twist to this sad, macabre tale is that the basement that was once a morgue was turned into the Museum of Death in 1995. Owners James Healy and Cathee Shultz created a museum dedicated to death in all its forms. From Tibetan burial displays to artwork by serial killers, it was one bizarre display of a fascination. It operated in the building for some years before moving up to North Hollywood where it is open to this day. I would only recommend going there if you wish a truly hard dose of reality, and tell most to avoid it.

It was James Healy who brought the tale of Tebbutt to "life," for he told many of his strange paranormal encounters while working in the museum. Healy often reported phantom footsteps downstairs as well as objects moved from their original locale.

On the street level of the building there is restaurant space. Over the years, I have watched several different establishments come and go. When I first started to investigate the Marin Building it was a Mexican restaurant and the owners there experienced so much phenomena, that when I first inquired, they were relieved that they had someone to share their stories with. The owner gave me a tour through the kitchen and I spoke to the staff who had encounters with what may be the spirit of Tebbutt. Plants were displaced and glasses were broken at the new bar that was installed downstairs in the basement. Even some of the female staff experienced having their hair pulled.

When we went behind the restaurant, the owner showed me a narrow set of stairs leading down into the dark of the night. When my colleague and I went downstairs, we noticed a small set of doors leading into the basement. The owner thought they were just windows. What she didn't realize was that they were not windows, but doors where the bodies were discreetly taken down into the morgue. When I informed her what they were, she was obviously disturbed. Her sole office window was a passageway for the newly dead.

Perhaps Tebbutt still walks the rooms and passageways of the old Marin. A sad soul, who after losing all he loved dear and in failing health, went out the only way he knew how. If you find yourself enjoying a meal at the restaurant on the street level of the Marin, just remember that the chair across from you might not be as empty as you think.

VISITOR INFORMATION

Marin Building
548-554 5th Avenue
San Diego, CA 92101

Several businesses are located here now.

CHAPTER FIVE

THE MELTING POT

JULIAN HOTEL

ALBERT ROBINSON

Albert Robinson walks the halls of his beloved home and hotel in the old mining town of Julian in the mountains east of San Diego. Even in death, he may continue to show his love for the venture he tried so hard to bring to fruition. His presence has been felt for years at the beautiful and charming Julian Hotel, the oldest continuously operating hotel in Southern California. Stories abound of a spectral presence: Menus flying off tables, the smell of lingering cigar smoke, billowing curtains and, the one that amuses me the most, flaming balls of light are all attributed to the ghost of Albert Robinson. Whether you believe Albert haunts the historic site or not, I leave up to you, but I'll definitely tell you why he *doesn't* haunt it.

If you ever visit the town of Julian, you are in for an experience that's hard to explain. It's not like other mining towns such as Virginia City or Tonopah. Instead of saloons and bordellos, you have fruit farmers and gold mines that represent the peak of the Southern California Gold Rush. You'll find rustic Victorian buildings filled with antique shops, souvenir stores, and, of course, apple pie. To say that Julian has a fascination with the apple would be an understatement. People come from all over Southern California for the pies and other apple products.

Historic Julian Hotel.

But a little over a hundred years ago, people flocked to Julian for a different reason—the sweet smell of gold.

In late 1869, Fred Coleman, an African-American who lived with an Indian family on Volcan Mountain, made an accidental discovery. While watering his mule at a streambed near what is now the town of Wynola, he spotted a glimmer in the water of what is now called Coleman Creek, and discovered placer gold. Having worked the gold fields of Northern California for some time before making his way south, Fred knew the precious mineral when he saw it. He established a mining district and began placer mining. Soon, others came and set up their sluice boxes seeking their fortune.

Among these miners were two sets of brothers, all cousins—Drury Bailey and his brothers, Frank and James, along with Mike and Webb Julian. All former confederate soldiers, they traveled their way west looking to escape the horrors of war and start over. Following the stream up into the nearby hills, they camped at the base of some small mountains and started looking for quartz deposits that may have harbored gold. On February 20, 1870, Drury discovered a quartz ledge and filed the first mining claim in the area, naming it the "Warrior's Rest." With word of gold in the hills, miners came from all over to try their hand at this newfound gold merely a day's ride from bustling San Diego.

The small encampment soon became a tent city, and when more and more quartz gold was discovered in the area, permanent wooden structures were built. This shanty of a camp became a full-fledged town seemingly overnight. It got the name Julian from Drury Bailey, who named it after his cousin, Mike Julian. Mike ran the claims office for a while and pushed a lot of the early Julian claims through. He also established the first Julian school board. He didn't stay in Julian long, though, and after a few years, left for San Diego and later made his way up the coast where he lived out his remaining years. The town of Julian wasn't the only mining town in the area, but it was the only one to survive. Why? Because after the gold rush subsided, the residents found a new trade: agriculture. And the rest is, well, history.

Albert Robinson was one of those men who came to Julian looking for his way in the world. Contrary to numerous websites and two books on the subject, Albert was not a victim of prejudice by any means. I used to give regular historic tours of the town of Julian, and one thing was certain, the town was a virtual melting pot. There were immigrants from all over, including Europeans from Germany and France, Russians, Native Americans, Mexicans, African-Americans, and Chinese looking for fortune.

According to a local census in the 1880s, a large portion of African-Americans were residing in the township of Julian and contributed greatly to the history there. In addition to discovering gold in the region, Fred Coleman established a toll road from Santa Ysabel to Julian through an agreement with the County of San Diego. America Newton homesteaded about eighty acres, and, for nearly a century, the stretch of highway that passes near her house has been called America's Grade. Albert's father-in-law was the first African-American to become a jury member in San Diego County.

In *Last Known Address: The Story of the Julian Cemetery*, author David Lewis, himself a fourth generation resident of Julian, states that Albert Robinson first arrived in San Diego County around 1870 and was associated with Major Levi Chase, a prominent land owner in the El Cajon area. Robinson worked his way up to Julian and patented 160 acres of land southwest of Julian in 1881. In 1886, he married Margaret Tull, daughter of Susan Tull.

Julian Pioneer Cemetery.

The Robinson's first business was a small restaurant that they opened using some of their own money and borrowing the rest. They struggled like many in the blossoming mining town, but gained an excellent reputation for both cooking and hospitality. In 1897, the restaurant expanded, and on the same site, they started the construction of a larger wooden structure that would become the Hotel Robinson. Albert died in that hotel in 1915, well respected and loved by many. Margaret continued operating the hotel until 1921, when she sold it to a local mining engineer. She retired and spent her remaining days in San Diego.

The ghost story surrounding Albert Robinson and the Julian Hotel is disturbing. In the books I read, including Gail White's book on "historic" haunts, as well as Robert Wlodarski's *Bottles of Boos* that covers haunted inns and restaurants, they depict the town as a racist community. I read many times over that, after Albert died, he was not allowed to be buried in the whites-only Julian Cemetery and that he had to be "buried with his own kind" at a separate cemetery down the hill. Supposedly, it's this "final indignation" that causes Albert to haunt his old hotel.

All one has to do to disprove this is to simply visit the Julian Cemetery where you will see quite plainly the grave of Albert Robinson, as well as the grave of his mother-in-law, and many other people who are not "white." When I contacted

Entrance to the Julian Cemetery.

author David Lewis, also the caretaker of the cemetery, and mentioned the articles that were written about Albert, he was happy to not only show me Albert's grave, but also those of other African-Americans who shaped Julian's history, including America Newton's grave, which, unlike the others, faces west towards her homestead. In Lewis' book on the Julian Cemetery, he references the diary of Thomas Wood, one of the first preachers in the Julian area who presided over Albert's funeral in 1915, and noted in it is that Albert was buried next to Wood's step-daughter, Martha. Wood was not African-American.

Another outlandish claim is that Albert's ghost prompted "concerned citizens of Julian to ask for an exorcism to be performed on the hotel." I checked with both the Julian Pioneer Museum as well as the Julian Historical Society and both had never heard of this story and found it absurd. Kay Sterner, the parapsychologist who first determined ghosts at the Whaley House, claimed to have performed exorcisms all around San Diego County. But there is no documentation of such a visit to the Julian Hotel nor had any of the old-timers ever heard of her.

I'm not sure if Albert haunts the halls of his beloved hotel, keeping an eye on things and making sure that the hospitality that it was once known for continues. In my opinion, if there is any injustice in this, it's from the sources that accused a town of racism. I haven't found where that story originated, but with little effort, it can be easily discounted.

VISITOR INFORMATION

JULIAN HOTEL

2032 Main Street, P.O. Box 1856, Julian, CA 92036
(760) 765-0201
www.julianhotel.com/

EAGLE-HIGH PEAK MINE

One true historic haunt may be found at the Eagle-High Peak Mine, located just a few blocks off Main Street in Julian. I spoke to many locals, including the owner, and had read about some paranormal activity in the old mine that was originally worked in the 1870s through 1939. This well-producing mine is also known for one of the worst disasters in the history of the mining district.

WILLIAM BOSWELL AND SIDNEY PETIT

On January 8, 1906, William Boswell, who worked as the superintendent of the Helvetia Mine and High Peak Mines, along with miner Sidney Petit, traveled into the mine to look at some reported cave-in activity. While examining the damage, a massive cave-in occurred and Petit was crushed instantly, while Boswell managed to get himself pinned upright next to a wooden brace and was crushed against it while he waited for rescue. I read that the wives of the men were waiting outside while the miners struggled to dig the two men out. When Petit's crushed and mangled body was retrieved, they took Boswell's wife away in fear of what her husband must look like in all the carnage.

Boswell was recovered and lingered in bed for several days before he finally expired from the internal injuries he sustained. Petit was buried in the Julian Cemetery while Boswell was boxed up and his wife traveled north with his coffin to Los Angeles for burial. Perhaps Boswell and Petit remember the tragedy all too well and remind visitors touring the historic (and very safe) Eagle-High Peak Mine that our time may come a lot sooner than we expect. A cool breeze when there should be none, an icy cold hand resting on your shoulder—all may be signs that these miners keep vigil here until the end of time.

VISITOR INFORMATION

EAGLE-HIGH PEAK MINE

2320 C Street, Box 624, Julian, CA 92036
(760) 765-0036

Eagle Peak/High Peak Mine entrance.

JULIAN JAIL

If you cannot stand the idea of being inside a mountain buried under tons of rock, I can also suggest investigating the jail on the edge of town. The old Julian Jail is a hallmark of days gone by. It's a stout one-story stone structure with a rusty, heavy iron door which you can open and walk around the two individually walled-off cells. The walking room around the cells provided a double layer of protection, not just to keep the convicts in, but to keep others out as well.

The jail has been in exactly the same place since the 1870s, but the jail you see there today is the latest version of it from the turn of the century. The previous two had been made out of wood and one suffered from a fire. The reason they made the stone one is simple: The stone finally made the structure permanent, thus allowing things like plumbing to be installed.

But one little thing they don't mention in the tourist guide is that the jail itself was the sight of several lynchings. I found records from many historic newspaper clips, as well as other documents, that describe the horrors of vigilante justice. A man who stole another man's horse saddle and trappings was locked up one night in the wooden jail, and was found dead right outside the jail beaten to death. Another account was of a prisoner locked up and found the next morning with his hands tied behind his back, swinging from a noose inside his very cell, the rope tied off at the rafters above. The coroner came in and ruled it a suicide. These accounts were very rare and hardly the definition of justice in this small town, but happen, they did.

I've come across others interested in investigating the paranormal and the number one place we can agree on within the town itself is the jail. It seethes something that's hard to describe. It's fascinating from a historical perspective, but when you spend time alone inside, there's a feeling of oppression and dread that's hard to ignore.

VISITOR INFORMATION

JULIAN JAIL

Corner of C and Fourth Streets, Julian, CA

CHAPTER SIX

THE PERFECT HAUNTED HOUSE

VILLA MONTEZUMA

You don't have to travel to the East Coast or Europe for a taste of the truly Gothic; you only need to go to the charming community of Sherman Heights. Perched on a hill like one of its own disturbing gargoyles is the Villa Montezuma, a crown jewel of Victorian architecture. From its first resident, mystery has been attached to this mansion including suicide, scandal, ruin, and disappearances, so much so that many refer to the Villa as not just haunted but cursed.

Stories abound from music being heard playing from inside the house, even though no one is clearly home or stained glass portraits that appear to age over the years. There is a tale of a butler who hanged himself in the tower and people say that they can see his face in the window on occasion. EVPs and orbs have been experienced throughout the interior and exterior of the grounds. What would one expect from a home in which one owner allegedly channeled the dead? But as one of my coworkers once said:

> The Villa Montezuma is not haunted… It's enchanted.

The Villa Montezuma today.

BENJAMIN HENRY JESSE FRANCIS SHEPARD

The main source behind the legend is the man for whom the house was built. Benjamin Henry Jesse Francis Shepard was born on September 18, 1848, in Birkenhead, England. In 1849, Shepard's family moved across the Atlantic and settled in Sangamon County, Illinois. Between the years of 1859-1862, the family moved to St. Louis and young Jesse became the page for General John C. Fremont, who would make quite a name for himself, not just in the Civil War, but also in the exploration of the American West.

It is believed that while in St. Louis, Shepard acquired rudimentary piano lessons. According to the legend of his "otherworldly" piano playing, certain sources claim he had no formal training, while Shepard himself claimed that he did not learn in "the usual way" but was instead "guided."

In 1863-1867, he honed his musical talent while staying with family members in Niagara Falls. By 1868, Shepard began giving music recitals in New York, Baltimore, and Boston. In 1869, he traveled alone to Europe and played in the salons of London and Paris. In 1871, Shepard arrived in St. Petersburg, Russia, where he spent the winter being instructed by famous Spiritualists in the area, and it is here where many believed he started practicing séances.

In 1874, Shepard returned to the United States under the supervision of Madame H.P. Blavatsky and was giving séances at her retreat in Chittenden, Vermont. Blavatsky was one of the primary founders of a spiritual movement known as Theosophy, which spoke of a Universal Truth in all religions, karma, and reincarnation. Shepard would later carry that philosophy into his own writings and lectures as well. It was through Blavatsky and her circle that he honed his skills as a medium.

From 1875-1886, there is not much documentation about Shepard's life. We do know that he lived in San Francisco, Australia, London, Paris, and Chicago, where he met his secretary and life-long friend, Lauritz Tonner. Here I would like to touch lightly on the relationship between Shepard and Tonner. There is speculation by many that they were lovers, and they may have been, but we simply don't know. During this time, homosexuality was frowned upon by the Victorian society and was in fact illegal, punishable by prison. So if they were involved in that way, they kept it a secret from the public. The only reason I mention it at all is because of the rumors that surround the man and I simply wish to put them to rest. In the end, we don't know, we probably never will, and even if he was, it doesn't matter.

In 1887, two wealthy ranchers and brothers, William and John High, wanted to lure Shepard to San Diego, entranced by his Spiritualism and European gentility. The ultimate bait was a house to be built for him so he could entertain the city's elite. San Diego was going through a huge economic boom due to a gold rush in the hills of Julian, the arrival of the railroad, and some of the wealthiest and most notable personalities on the West Coast lived there. The community, later called Sherman Heights, was chosen and the famous architects Comstock and Trotsche went to work with the aid of Shepard's vision.

Although the house was christened the Villa Montezuma, it was also called "The Palace of the Arts." Its unusual design counteracts most of Victorian society and even the cutting edge of Queen Anne architecture with a Russian onion top-domed tower and multiple windows of highly decorative art glass represents not just authors and artists whom Shepard admired, but figures in Christian and Pagan mythos. Gargoyles and dragons sit about the roof of the house, used traditionally in architecture as a protection from evil spirits. On the top of the house is a weathervane with a winged serpent entwined around it.

Dragon weathervane on top of Villa Montezuma. Decorative piece or protective talisman?

Most everything in the design of the house was able to be prefabricated and moved onsite. All but one of the fireplaces were purchased out of a catalog and installed. And yes, keeping in Gothic tradition, there were even secret passages. The fireplace in the parlor lifted up at the mantle and you could crawl into a hidden section of the house as well as into the rafter area between the floors above the music room.

It was while he was in San Diego that Shepard discovered a new talent: writing. He began writing articles and essays for a monthly publication called *The Golden Era*, which was started in San Francisco in 1852. Later, in 1887, he moved to San Diego after city officials enticed the publication's owner, Herr Wagner, with a $5,000 subsidy. *The Golden Era* produced some of the earliest writings of Joaquin Miller, Ada Clare, and, most notably, Mark Twain.

If or how many séances he conducted in San Diego is unknown, but Shepard was known to give lavish parties and concerts at his home that lasted long into the night. He claimed many psychic gifts throughout his career, including mystic, medium, and prophet. Was Jesse Shepard a gifted medium able to communicate with the dead? Were the lavish piano chords played not by him, but by the dead playing through him? Those who saw his concerts frequently used terms such as "ethereal and otherworldly" to describe them.

Sam High, a nephew of the High Brothers, described one of Shepard's concerts that he attended in a *San Diego Union* article dated July 20, 1913:

> Everybody gathered in the music room and sat in chairs facing the piano, which was in one corner. Shepard stood by the piano, with his back to the keys. Then the lights were put out. In a moment the most wonderful music started, first the piano alone and then far off what sounded like a choir of voices coming down the street. The voices came nearer and nearer and the volume of sound grew louder until finally it seemed to be right in the room. Then in a few minutes it began to die out, gradually growing fainter and fainter until it was gone and only the piano was heard. Then the lights were turned on and it was all over and there was Shepard standing and bowing to the audience.

San Diego became a turning point for Shepard—he concentrated on his writing, converted to Catholicism, and allegedly turned his back on Spiritualism, although some of his later books featured occult themes. Shepard also confessed to Father Antonio Ubach, a well-known priest who presided over Shepard's conversion to Catholicism, that large portions of his séances were faked. This was quite common during the Victorian era. Even if one was a talented psychic or medium, it was still required to "put on a show." What if he didn't receive any messages that day? Something had to be produced. It's like watching paranormal shows on television today. All is grand as long as EVPs are being recorded, pictures taken, and beds shaken. But the moment something doesn't happen...well, who is going to watch *that*?

Portrait of Jesse Shepard painted while he was in St. Petersburg in 1872. Portrait done by Mathieu Geslin, court painter for the Czar of Russia.

After a trip to France in 1888, Shepard decided to leave San Diego and return to Europe to pursue a literary career. His first published work appeared in 1889 and was titled *Modern Mysticism*—so much for his rebuking of Spiritualism. In 1896, Shepard changed his name to Francis Grierson. Francis was his middle name and Grierson his mother's maiden name. One of his books was titled *The Valley of Shadows*, an autobiographical account of growing up in pre-Civil War Illinois. That book was considered a minor classic of its time and is still in print.

In 1919, Shepard lectured in the subject of Theosophy in Toronto for a time before moving to Los Angeles to live out his remaining years. Supported by Tonner, Shepard struggled financially and strove for a comeback that never materialized.

He found a Guardian Angel in the form of a female author and poet by the name of Zona Gale. She took pity on his plight and sent him some money while she arranged a benefit concert in which he would perform and hopefully raise some funds. Shepard pawned all of his treasures that he acquired from his travels of Europe and the last thing he sold was a gold watch given to him by Royalty.

1908 postcard featuring the Villa Montezuma. This is more how it looked while Jesse Shepard lived there.

The benefit concert took place on May 29, 1927 in Los Angeles at the home of a friend. Shepard arrived late as always, charmed the people in attendance and, despite being 79 years old, played the piano like he was a young man again. He played for what seemed like forever and concluded the evening with one of his most famous pieces entitled "The Egyptian March." When he struck the final chord, he bowed his head. As the thunder of applause settled down, he did not move. It was soon discovered by Tonner that Shepard was dead, at the piano, his fingers resting on the final chord of his most celebrated piece.

Shepard died as he lived, in style. The cause of his death was a heart attack due to malnutrition. In essence, he starved to death. He was buried in Los Angeles under the name Francis Grierson. Tonner would follow him to the grave almost exactly 20 years later on May 27, 1947. After forty-two years of service

Interior of Villa during Shepard's occupancy.

1876 Steinway piano on display today at Mission Inn in Riverside.

and friendship, Tonner was laid to rest in Inglewood Park Cemetery where his epitaph reads "Devoted Friend."

Gale was friends with Frank Miller, the owner of the famous Mission Inn in Riverside. Their correspondence reveals that they had made an agreement to raise funds for Shepard so that he and Tonner could summer at the luxury resort hotel. It would have been a generous offer for the struggling author given his current living conditions. But probably most tempting was the opportunity to play daily at the classic 1876 Steinway piano that sat in the hotel lobby (and still does to this day). Upon Shepard's death, Frank Miller sent a telegram to Gale that read simply this:

> Francis Grierson died last night. I have sent Dewitt down a few weeks ago with an earnest invitation for him to come to the Mission Inn as my guest, with the same thoughts that you have written me. It is well for the dear man to go as he did.

I could almost leave the story of the house alone, and many would say it could be haunted by Jesse Shepard, though he spent so little time there, and after he left, never returned. Tonner commented on the home only once, in a newspaper article in 1927. He spoke fondly of the Villa and commented on how lovely the shrubs and rose bushes must be now, for he and Shepard planted them together there in the backyard. This home was Jesse Shepard's. It was one of the grandest things he ever owned, and to my knowledge the only property he ever held.

But the owners who possessed the Villa after Shepard left their own mark on the dark history of the mansion and it's their misfortune that has led some to refer to the Villa Montezuma as cursed.

THE VILLA CHANGING HANDS

The man who purchased it completely furnished from Shepard for $29,000, D.D. Dare, has his own shadowy past. David Dickey Dare was the vice-president of the new California National Bank which had considerable assets. He was also the principle backer in a fledgling cable car company starting up in San Diego. Dare lived in the house for only a short time, while his own Brownstone mansion was being built in an area now known as Banker's Hill. Dare entertained guests in the Villa and when his own home, Castle Dare, was completed he put the Villa on the market and sold it to H.P. Palmerston for $30,000. Palmerston moved into the Villa Montezuma and bought the Horton House Hotel and heavily invested in D.D. Dare's bank and cable car company.

What Palmerston and the rest of San Diego didn't know is that D.D. Dare, as well as J.W. Collins, the cashier of the bank, were professional con men. Dare and Collins both moved to San Diego from Cheyenne, Wyoming where they ran a hardware business and had opened the Cheyenne National Bank. Before that, Dare was a modest sign painter and photographer with more ambition and gall than anything else. They transformed themselves into banking tycoons and took the booming city by storm. Opening the California National Bank and California Savings Bank, they possibly operated a type of Ponzi scheme selling bank shares to raise funds.

But one day, in November 1891, the doors to California National Bank remained closed. Dare disappeared with a briefcase full of money, first to Europe and later resurfaced around the Mediterranean. The two San Diego banks closed with shortfalls of about $800,000 and the Cheyenne bank closed a few days later. A domino effect occurred with the cable car shutting down, too. His business partner, J.W. Collins, obviously didn't get the memo that it was time to rob their own bank and get out of town. Collins was placed under house arrest at the Hotel Brewster where he resided. U.S. Marshal George E. Gard had charge of Collins and gave him free rein of the hotel knowing he wasn't going anywhere.

Collins had suffered his own tragedy in the recent years when his wife and children were killed when the yacht they were on capsized off the coast of Pt. Loma. He never left his rooms at the Brewster. When told he would be moved to Los Angeles for trial, he asked to use the restroom where he put a pistol in his mouth and pulled the trigger.

Palmerston, like many others, were financially ruined by Dare's "disappearance" and the closure of the cable car company. Palmerston had taken out a mortgage of $15,000 with the California Mortgage Loan and Trust Company (of which Dare was part owner) and the Villa was foreclosed on in 1893. The house was sold at auction for the price of $18,000 to one of the mortgage company officers, Mr. Hiram Duryea.

A few years later, Duryea sold the mansion for a mere $10,000 to Dr. George Calmus who lived at the Villa with his wife and mother-in-law for six years. According to legend, one day he went to work and just disappeared. Emma Calmus spoke about the house and the disappearance of her husband in the 1913 *San Diego Union* article. She said Dr. Calmus began speculating in Los Angeles real estate, grew reckless, lost everything they had, and went away, disappearing entirely. This led some people to speculate that the curse of the Villa had claimed Calmus, when actually it was probably just a bad marriage. Calmus headed to the Northern California gold fields, appearing in the 1920 U.S. Census for San Andreas, Calaveras County and later back in Los Angeles as a guest at the Van Nuys Hotel in 1930.

The house went into foreclosure, went to George Sinclair and was used as a rental property. Two of the tenants were Mr. and Mrs. George W. Montgomery and they were known to give readings and séances in the house between the years of 1906-1909. By now, the Villa had acquired an interesting reputation for being a haunted house and one that brought bad luck to whoever owned it. The Montgomerys couldn't pay their rent and had to vacate the Villa.

The "curse" appeared to have been lifted when Frank and Georgia Lynch purchased the Villa in 1909 and restored it to the beauty of its original owner. Frank was one of the owners of the Benson Lumber Company, one of the largest lumber manufacturers in the West, and they lived happily in the Villa for over thirty-three years until their deaths in 1942.

The *San Diego Union* article dated July 20, 1913 was entitled, "Villa Montezuma, Temple of Art and Occultism, for Years Brought Ill Luck to All Who Bought It; Now Happy Home With Evil Spell Broken" and appeared while the Lynch family occupied the Villa. The article recounted the past owners, but added the High Brothers to the mix. Their nephew, Sam High, accused Shepard of financially ruining the "simple fruit peddlers" by hypnotizing the brothers into funding the ornate mansion and the entertainer's lavish lifestyle, while the "two poor old uncles" drove by in their little wagon, peddling vegetables from door to door.

However, an article on Shepard which appeared in the 1970 summer edition of the *Journal of San Diego* gives a great defense of Shepard and dismisses the notion that the High Brothers suffered financially or were victims. The High Brothers owned thousands of acres throughout San Diego County and William's 1894 obituary describes him as "well-to-do."

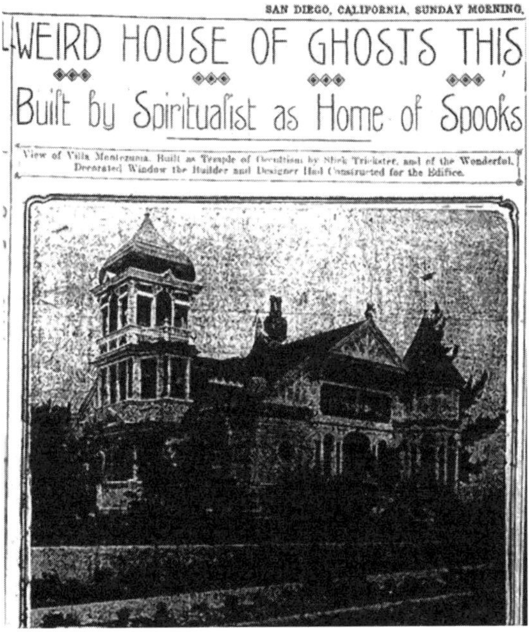
SAN DIEGO, CALIFORNIA, SUNDAY MORNING.

WEIRD HOUSE OF GHOSTS THIS

Built by Spiritualist as Home of Spooks

View of Villa Montezuma, Built as Temple of Occultism by Slick Trickster, and of the Wonderful Decorated Window the Builder and Designer Had Constructed for the Edifice.

1913 *San Diego Union* article on the "curse" of the Villa Montezuma.

In 1948, the Villa was purchased by Edward Campbell, who had the house in his possession for only four months. Most of that time was spent digging in the backyard looking for buried treasure. Unsuccessful, he sold the house to other investors.

In 1950, the Villa was sold to a retired engineer by the name of Carl Yaeger and his wife, a former silent screen actress. After several years in the house together, Carl died, leaving his wife to care for the sadly deteriorating mansion. There were questions of Mrs. Yaeger's mental stability and stories abound of how she used to frighten neighborhood children. The community was becoming inhabited by primarily Latino families and the children referred to Mrs. Yaeger as a "bruja," Spanish for *witch*.

In 1968, the home was sold for $12,000 to John and Juanita Finn. The sale was contested for some time by the relatives of Mrs. Yaeger due to her mental state at the time of sale. In 1970, The Superior Court voided the sale and put the set market value of the home at $26,000. A group of five friends, who were local history buffs and preservationists, each pitched in money to purchase the home with the intention of turning it into a museum. It was lovingly restored and stewardship was given to the San Diego Historical Society. The Villa Montezuma opened to the public in November 1972.

In the 1980s, a fire, believed to have been caused by a space heater accidently left on, ravaged a goodly portion of the music room and the floors above it. The firefighters in the area knew the Villa well and were given free tours of it frequently, and so when they arrived, they fought the flames with preservation as a priority. Not a single stained glass was destroyed and later all the wood was lovingly restored and reproduced.

AN AUTHOR'S PERSPECTIVE

The mansion is a true mystery house. I first became intimate with it many years ago while working for a tour company in San Diego. From then I was hooked and would come back for a guided tour on my days off from one of the docents there. After leaving the tour company, I was hired by the San Diego Historical Society and the Villa Montezuma became a second home for me where I would spend up to ten hours a day, giving tours and overseeing the upkeep and maintenance of the museum. This gave me quite the edge when I became interested in the paranormal. When I was not running tours and other duties, the house was mine to explore.

I used to arrive early for tours, with my token Starbuck's coffee in hand, and just lie down face-up in the center of the music room. As the morning sun crept over the neighboring houses and the light struck the stained-glass windows throughout the room, a cascade of reds and blues would pour through that portion of the house that would put anyone in a state of awe. You could hear the house breathing as the wood warmed in the sun. You could almost feel Jesse Shepard here once again. It was no wonder fellow docents called it "enchanted."

Because of the paranormal history associated with the Villa, it is a magnet for ghost tours and paranormal investigators, but there is very little known about the house from a paranormal standpoint. Very few people have been allowed to spend time in the Villa for the sole purpose of exploring the phenomena that has been reported to allegedly take place there, and I don't blame the San Diego Historical Society one bit. It's a museum dedicated not just to one mystic's life, but to the opulence of high Victorian society; it is not a paranormal cash cow spook house.

There are many stories of supposed paranormal activity associated with the mansion, including the famous battery draining of all equipment on occasion with film crews. There was an EVP circulating for a while with a woman's voice. One of the more interesting stories about the Villa came from a former coworker who used to work for Old Town Trolley's Ghost and Gravestones guided tour. She used to wait along with a museum docent for the house for the evening tour to arrive. She would tell the stories associated with the house and then the visitors would be allowed to walk through a couple of rooms before they were ushered back onto the trolley for their next destination. One night, right after the tour left, she looked out the lace curtain at the front door and spotted a very tall man in a gray suit on the front porch looking out onto the street. She thought that it was someone left behind from the tour, but when she opened the front door to see if she could help the stranger, he was gone.

Even I have had a couple of encounters that have made me a believer that all may not be as it seems at the Villa Montezuma. Sadly though, some of the

Salon window featuring Shepard's favorite authors.

Interior of Villa Montezuma Music Room, Sappho window.

Window named Occident, meaning west, showing Shepard's western influences.

Window named Orient, meaning east, Shepard's eastern influences.

stories associated with the Gothic mansion are completely false and stain the history of this beautiful home. And those are the ones that get published over and over again as truth. One such story is of a butler who allegedly hanged himself in the tower of the Villa and now haunts the home. It is said that on certain nights you can see the tormented young man's face staring down at you and that his apparition has been spotted in the tower.

From a historic standpoint, Jesse and Lauritz never employed a butler in their short time at the Villa, let alone one that was depressed enough from a lost love to commit suicide there. There are no newspaper accounts of any such suicide or body being discovered inside the Villa. Architecturally, the ceiling of the tower really isn't that high with no load-bearing structure within it. The dome is technically hollow. It's a smooth surface with nothing to attach a rope to but a simple light fixture which certainly wouldn't support the weight of a person.

Another ghost story circulating out there has the most natural explanation. One of the stained-glass windows in the music room is that of Peter Paul Rubens, the famous seventeenth-century painter. Several websites and books claim that supernatural forces are at work and that his beard is graying over the years and, you know, it is. But what the tale doesn't take into account is that all of the portraits in the house are not stained glass in the facial areas, but painted glass. It's not glass fading in color, it's paint. Black paint turns to gray after years of exposure to the sun.

By the way, the portraits in the windows are magnificent, done by John Mallon in San Francisco. It is believed that he used photographs to aid the painting on the glass, but no one truly knows. He took the true secret of his brilliance to the grave, which is far more fascinating. The art glass is believed to be one of the largest amounts of residential art glass on the West Coast.

There is also a story circulating that there is a certain location in the house where no plants will grow and prosper. I guess the only way you can actually counteract that is to actually visit the house. There is a corner of the house, a small conservatory, for the purpose of placing houseplants. Shepard may have designed it himself. It's a beautiful octagonal corner with a tile floor and large windows of plain and art glass. The stained-glass windows in the conservatory are labeled for the four seasons with ornate flowers decorating each. A red glass lamp that could be lowered by counterweighted chain hangs from the center. I can only assume that this is where the plants do not prosper. The rest of the house is rather dark throughout between the rich woods and the art glass. The conservatory itself, though made for the purpose of helping plants prosper only gets a limited amount of light during the day. Perhaps it was an architectural oversight. The design of the house as a whole is more about form than function, and maybe the conservatory can be just added to the list.

Villa Montezuma Conservatory, location where plants are rumored to die.

Another misconception that I discovered is that Jesse died in the house. Several San Diego ghost tours visit the Villa, pointing out the unique and hauntingly beautiful architectural features of the building as well as giving a basic history. One tour I came across suggested that Jesse Shepard himself may haunt the house. I'll buy that, given the history of the man and his supposed talents. But at least one tour proceeds to tell you that Shepard died in the house, at the piano, of tuberculosis. After the tour, I asked the guide why he told his guests such a fallacy, explaining that he died in Los Angeles of angina brought on by malnutrition, not tuberculosis. His answer was that it made a better story. History about a great man had just been changed because he thought that you might have been more entertained if you were lied to.

Another fallacy is that Mrs. Yaeger died in the house as well and that no one found her for weeks and was only discovered due to the smell of her decomposing body. Apparently, the descendants of Mrs. Yaeger heard that one, too, and were none too pleased.

Today, ownership of the historic home has been returned to the City of San Diego and the house is currently closed awaiting funding for necessary repairs to the foundation. If you get a chance, drive by the Villa Montezuma on a crisp fall evening. The gingerbread siding is holding up nicely and the gargoyles and serpents on the roof still keep a vigilant protective eye upon this wonderful mysterious abode.

Is the Villa Montezuma, as the 1913 newspaper article claimed, a "weird house built as home of spooks"? Perhaps the best explanation comes from William High in a letter to the editor of the *San Diego Sun* in April 1888:

> My attention has been called to certain rumors, circulated by gossips and busybodies, to the effect that Villa Montezuma was built as a kind of "spiritual temple" for the accommodation of spiritualists, and for the holding of spiritual séances. Villa Montezuma was intended for a private home, belongs to Jesse Shepard, and is therefore exclusively a private residence. Séances are not held in Mr. Shepard's house. The subject of spiritism [sic] is not touched upon by the numerous visitors who call there.

VISITOR INFORMATION

VILLA MONTEZUMA HOUSE MUSEUM

1925 K Street, San Diego, CA 92102
www.villamontezumamuseum.org

(At publication, the Villa is closed. For visits other than a drive by, check the website.)

CHAPTER SEVEN

JOURNEY OF DEATH

Stories of this kind reveal a strong bond between man and his surroundings, and disclose the trend of thought that gropes for a haven on the border of the unknown.

~Phillip Bailey *Golden Mirages*

THE GREAT ANZA-BORREGO DESERT

Ghost stories and legends rule the local desert. A spectral horse, an eight-foot skeleton, and even a Lady in White grace the haunted history of the great Anza-Borrego Desert, the largest state park in California. What do you expect when the main route across the desert was known as "El Camino del Diablo," the Devil's Highway, and travel along it was referred to as the Journey of Death?

The first Europeans to travel through this region were Spanish soldiers looking for deserters. The Mormon Battalion, as well as the great scout, Kit Carson, crossed this portion of the desert when war broke out between Mexico and the United States. After the tragedy of the Donner Party in 1846, travelers became wary of crossing through the Sierra Nevada Mountains into California and began looking for an alternate southern route. They discovered the long, desolate passage that stretched from Fort Yuma to San Diego. But although it was free of snow, it proved to be even more deadly. Pioneer traveler Bayard Taylor described it as "a country of burning salt plains and shifting hills of sand, whose only signs of human visitation are the bones of animals and men scattered along the trails that cross it."

From this route came many legends and folklore, including gunfights over buried treasure, lost mines, Peg Leg's golden nuggets, and murdering bandits. These tales of desperate men on the verge of starvation, dehydration, and exposure to the elements almost always ended in death. Sadly, from a historian's point of view there are a lack of physical resources to reference when investigating the stories of the mysteries of the Anza-Borrego. We have few written contemporary accounts and most were documented years after the events occurred. Several of the books actually contradict themselves and even the newspaper accounts are sketchy at best. Therefore, the ghost stories are best viewed primarily as folklore.

Traveling across the barren sands, the most precious commodity was water. Coldwater springs were rare throughout the Anza-Borrego Desert. But one such respite, Vallecito, which means "little valley" acquired a more sinister reputation. According to Phillip Bailey, author of *Golden Mirages*:

> An old, wise desert-man, now living in Julian, told me that no one who knew the story of Vallecito would sleep within its once-friendly walls.

Vallecito was first used by Spanish soldiers as a watering hole and place to cache supplies on their patrols. A small building was erected using large slabs of salt-grass sod cut from nearby thermal springs. From 1854 to 1857, Joseph Swycaffer and Samuel Warnock began carrying government dispatches and mail between Old Town San Diego and Fort Yuma, Arizona, traveling through Vallecito, which had been rebuilt by James R. Lassitor. In 1857, the Butterfield Mail Company established a stagecoach route that ran from St. Louis to San Francisco, passing through the Anza-Borrego Desert. Stage stations were built along the route approximately fifteen to twenty miles apart, and Vallecito was enlarged to accommodate guests.

The stagecoach line continued until 1861 with the beginning of the Civil War. The service was discontinued because the route traveled through both Union and Confederate states. Lassitor left his wife and stepson in charge of the station in 1864 and went to Arizona to do some prospecting. A year later, Lassitor headed home with $3,000-$4,000 in gold but was found murdered near the Gila River, the gold missing. Lassitor's widow and her recently widowed daughter stayed at Vallecito until mid-1866, when the station was sold to John Hart. Hart himself died a year later of what was called natural causes at the age of 31.

The stage station was held as a way stop for travelers until the train finally made its way out west and the stagecoach became obsolete. The station, being made out of sod in an adobe-like construction, fell into disrepair until reconstruction of it took place in 1934. The cemetery was all but gone, and so during the reconstruction, they rebuilt the cemetery with only three graves, even though I found records stating that several people died there. Two of those graves represent former stage station owners, John Hart and the ashes of James E. Mason who had settled at Vallecito in the 1870s. The other grave was constructed for The Lady in White, the most popular ghost story of the Anza-Borrego desert.

THE LADY IN WHITE

The most common telling of the story is this: In the late 1850s, a young woman was traveling across the desert by stagecoach on her way to get married in Sacramento. She became ill and her health continued to fail throughout the journey. By the time the stagecoach reached the Vallecito station, the fever had escalated. She was carried into the station and placed on a bed while Mrs. Lassitor attempted to lower the fever. Alas, nothing succeeded and she passed on to the next world.

The travelers and owners of the station were in mourning and decided to open her luggage in hopes of finding out more about her in order to send her belongings onward to family. They found within her possessions a beautiful white dress with delicate embroidery and beading, obviously her intended wedding dress. She was carefully dressed in it and buried at the small cemetery. Ever since, there have been reports of a ghost bride pacing nervously outside the station waiting for the stagecoach to take her to her lost love. I have spoken with park rangers who patrol the property, and while some hold an amount of levity to the story, others are just plain scared by it. My favorite part of the story is, for the most part, true.

The first tracing of the story I can find from something other than folklore is in *History of Julian,* a book published in 1969 by the Julian Historical Society. It has a small mention of a young woman by the name of Martha Ward who came to the Warner's Ranch area in the 1850s. She later married Joseph Swycaffer, the gentleman who had started the mail route across the desert through Vallecito. It states:

> Martha had crossed the plains and desert from Texas in a covered wagon train; her closest relative, a sister, had died at the Vallecito Stage Station en route, leaving her alone in this strange new country.

Members of the Ward family, living descendants of Martha Ward, are familiar with the story of the relative who died at Vallecito. After much research, I have found what may be the best identity for the Lady in White. First, the death took place in 1854, before Butterfield started its famous stagecoach line. But there was plenty of migration west, and Martha Ward is found in the 1850 U.S. Census living in Walker, Texas along with William and Mary Cummings, and their two small children. In a *Tribune-Sun* article dated July 25th, 1947, there is a mention of Martha Ward, her arrival to San Diego County, and her marriage to Joseph Swycaffer in 1857. In the article it notes:

> On Ward's trip from Texas, a daughter, Fannie Ward Cummings, succumbed to illness at Vallecito, a sunken wagonbed marking her grave.

Actually, it couldn't have been the young child, Frances "Fannie" Cummings, who died as she appeared a few years later in another U.S. Census living with her husband, Thomas Despain, father William and two small children. Frances "Fannie" Cummings died in 1928 and is buried at the Yuma Cemetery in Yuma, Arizona. William Cummings remarried in 1858, appeared in the 1860 U.S. Census living with his son, James Cummings, and died at the age of 69 in Mariposa, California, in 1894. The only person who disappears from all record is Mary Cummings, presumably Martha Ward's aunt or sister and the woman who is factually known to have died at Vallecito. But she was a young mother traveling with her family, not a mail-order bride.

According to *Anza-Borrego A to Z*, written by Diana Lindsay in 2001:

> Ward's aunt is most likely the "Lady in White" as there are no other records of a woman passenger dying at Vallecito. The only fact that is known is that Ward became an orphan when her aunt died.

So if the only known woman to have died at Vallecito was not en route to her fiancé in the gold fields, but a young mother traveling West with her family, who then is the Lady in White?

An article written in the *San Diego Union* dated December 2, 1934, may provide some answers. Restoration on the old stage station at Vallecito was underway and the headline reads, "Vallecito Ghost Legend Revived; Workman Quits." The article refers to:

> ...the legend that has persisted for years. There are old-timers who swear they have seen the ghost bride and who also have heard ghost horses galloping from the Cuyamacas and the whispered conversation of two men riders who always stop at the south door of the Vallecito station, but who just aren't there if some brave soul goes to investigate. They tell, too, of seeing dancing white lights through the darkness.

> Other old-timers scoff. It has been said that one woman once masqueraded as the ghost-bride. It seems her daughter had a suitor the mother didn't like, so mother took the moonlight ride on a black horse—and the young man hasn't been seen again.

At one time, in the mid-1860s, there was a mother and daughter living at Vallecito. After James Lassitor was murdered on his way back from Arizona, the station was inhabited for almost two years by Lassitor's widow, Sarah, and her daughter, Loduska Kimble, whose husband had also been recently murdered near Warner's Ranch. A ghostly bride is born.

STAGECOACH ROBBERIES

There are other ghosts who are said to haunt the stage station. One of the most colorful stories is that of two banditos. After they had robbed a stagecoach and hidden the loot, they retired to Vallecito for some rest and celebration. According to the story, a fight broke out between the two bandits over the division of money. The leader of the two quickly made up and apologized for the matter and stepped outside the station for a moment, promising to return quickly. Soon after, the large door of the stage station burst open and the leader rode into the stage station mounted on a white horse and shot his companion. As the dying bandit fell, he fired a shot which killed the leader. The white horse, spooked by the gunfire and death of its master, rode off into the night. Legend has it that around midnight, near where the stolen treasure was buried, a white ghost horse will appear.

People have reported seeing a white horse roaming the desert late at night near the old stage stop. In *Marshal South and the Ghost Mountain Chronicles*, published in 2005, Rider South recounted a time his mother and father camped overnight at Vallecito before the restoration. He wrote:

> They were sound asleep one night when they were awakened by the ghost of a big white horse. Tanya saw it but not Marshal. Needless to say, they fled and never wanted to sleep there again.

A fine story, but it does have its problems. There are several conflicts regarding a stagecoach robbery. Pioneer historian and newspaper owner, James Jasper, recounts in his 1934 memoirs a story entitled "The Battle of Vallecito" told to him in 1888 by Old Bill Smith, a stagecoach driver in Julian. According to Jasper, there had only been one raid on the stages west of the Colorado River and that was in the fall of 1858. Five bandits attacked the stagecoach and shots were fired. The driver instructed his three passengers to "shoot to kill." One bandit was killed along with one of the passengers before soldiers from Vallecito came to their rescue. According to Jasper, the dead passenger was planted in an Indian graveyard nearby and that's where his story ends. But an unsubstantiated claim later appeared in the October 1970 issue of *Desert* magazine which added that the next morning Old Bill was surprised that there were no prisoners. He questioned the corporal who smiled and replied, "Vallecito has no accommodations for prisoners—outside of the graveyard." I'm not sure where that additional information came from, but it makes a great footnote and, if true, adds four more bodies to the Vallecito cemetery.

Bailey's *Golden Mirages* from 1940 gives a more colorful version of the tale with four bandits robbing the stage just past Tres Palmas Spring of $65,000 before heading off to Vallecito. The stage driver fired a shot and brought down one of the bandits. When he went to examine the body, he discovered two dead bandits and surmised that the leader, who rode a great white horse, must have shot the other to avoid sharing the spoils. Bailey gives the leader the name O'Hara and even quotes the conversations the two bandits had at the Vallecito stage station. In this version, it says:

> He rode the big white horse up to the adobe stage station, kicked in the door, and took a shot at his brother, hitting him in the chest. As he wheeled his horse to go, the mortally wounded brother pulled his gun and shot O'Hara in back of the right ear.

That left a robbed stagecoach, four dead bandits, and a loose white horse.

There was either another stagecoach robbery which was not recorded, which is unlikely but possible, or somehow these two stories became one. While the White Horse of Vallecito has enthralled paranormal investigators, the lost $65,000 continues to entice treasure hunters to this day.

In his chapter entitled, "The Vallecito Ghosts", Jasper also recounts the story of two brothers-in-law, Buck and Roland (also read as Toland) who quarreled all the way from Texas and died at Vallecito in a double homicide. According to Jasper, the two men staged a duel there in 1870, both were killed, and supposedly stage an annual ghostly comeback on each recurring anniversary of the duel. In Judd Tripp's book, *Old Cattlemen of Anza Borrego*:

> The bodies of the victims to the shooting were buried in the little cemetery on the small hill to the east of the station, but after a time were moved to Julian.

David Lewis, who runs the historical Pioneer Cemetery in Julian, was not familiar with the story and doubts their burial there. If true, that adds two more bodies to Vallecito.

Vallecito stagecoach station exterior.

PHANTOM STAGECOACH

There is a tale of a phantom stagecoach that travels the "Camino del Diablo" through the Carrizo wash on its way to the Vallecito stagecoach station. I found several versions of the story, but in all its versions, it's roughly the same. A stagecoach laden with gold was making its way across the desert. Its last major stop before San Diego was Fort Yuma. The driver's attendant had fallen ill and the driver looked for a replacement guard to aid him in the final crossing of the desert. Finding no one and knowing that he was under a deadline, the driver continued on from Yuma into the darkness of the dangerous void. All went well until just shy of the Carrizo station, when the stage fell under an ambush. The driver pushed his animals onward but a single shot struck home and the driver slumped into his seat, the horses galloping on their own. Pulling into Carrizo Station, the stagecoach came to a stop as it normally would...the driver was dead.

The phantom stagecoach of Carrizo is said to have been seen by many campers who spend the night in the vicinity of the old Carrizo Station to the southeast of Vallecito. An old prospector in the area by the name of Charlie McCloud used to spin a yarn about seeing the phantom stagecoach. Charlie related this spectral

Vallecito graveyard rebuilt in 1934.

story to Bailey in *Golden Mirages*. Bailey came out to the ruins of the Carrizo stage station to interview McCloud, whom he knew would be camping there. It was there, that McCloud said he had spotted the phantom stagecoach as it made its way through the evening. Sometimes, but not always, it would leave its wagon wheel tracks in its wake. One morning, according to McCloud, he spotted something in the wagon tracks left by the coach. He reportedly held it up to Bailey to inspect. It was an 1830s gold piece.

Even though it is no longer there, the location of the San Felipe stage station supposedly holds a supernatural aura. The site for the station was built on the edge of a Native American village that the workers thought was abandoned, not realizing that the people in the area were migratory. After the station was built, the Indians returned and were appalled to see that the wooden stage station was built near their burial grounds.

SAN FELIPE STAGE STATION

The stage station itself has had its own tragedies, including murder and robbery, which both Jasper and Bailey refer to. Fred Grand had the lease on the San Felipe grant and kept the station in good condition until authorized to demolish it between 1888 and 1892. In *Anza-Borrego A to Z,* the place was supposedly haunted and that, according to local pioneers, Grand would never sleep there. Grand was later killed by his own wagon in a freak accident while hauling freight down the Banner Grade.

According to Bailey, two prospectors who had struck it rich, stopped in at the San Felipe stage station one night, late in the 1850s. A lone bandit came in and robbed the two miners, relieving them of their newfound wealth. The bandit sent the two men off into the desert and returned to the station about half an hour later. The hostler now recognized the bandit and made the mistake of calling him by name. The incensed bandit ordered the hostler outside to dig his own grave. But the man rushed the bandit, bringing the shovel down on his head just as the bandit fired his gun. Both bodies were discovered shortly thereafter by a traveler but there was no gold to be found.

Bailey claimed that there was a curse on the place and muffled voices and glimpses of ghostly shovels have been reported. Jasper also refers to:

> Traditions of a double murder and buried treasure linger there and the spot is still haunted by the credulous who come and dig about the old ruin in hope of unearthing a lost treasure.

If you want to visit the site today, travel from Julian down towards Borrego and stop at Scissors Crossing. There is a grove of trees off the side of the road by the San Felipe creek. The grove is all that remains of the old stage station, and the memories of greed and death.

In Gail White's book, *Haunted San Diego*, she writes about a house in the small town of Banner, which is situated between the town of Julian and the Anza-Borrego desert. Banner was once a boomtown like Julian, brimming with miners and merchants with gold on their mind. But like other towns in the area, the gold rush ended and the town was later washed away by a terrible flood and never recovered.

She tells a wonderful ghost story about a house in Banner and an old resident who lived there who simply went by the name "Arkansas." According to White's book, Arkansas moved into the old house in the hills and later left the house in complete terror. He was awakened at night by disembodied groaning and the sound of the stropping of a razor. After some time, the house fell into disrepair and the locals would come by and examine this haunted locale for their own entertainment. No one knows where that house was in Banner, for its long gone. And sadly, that's where White leaves it, but there is so much more to add.

You can find the source of the story in a *San Diego Union* article from September 18, 1874 entitled, "Haunted House in Banner City." It read:

> An unoccupied house situated in a picturesque grove of oaks, and formerly occupied as a store, is causing a sensation. Since the store was discontinued, a family moved in and remained about a month, but their peace was disturbed by strange carryings-on, and they left suddenly, picking up bag and baggage and not standing upon the order of going.
>
> The house was next occupied by a man named "Arkansas." Now Arkansas was not raised in the woods to be scared by an owl, but he couldn't stand that house of strange unearthly sounds that disturbed his sleep. The noise he complained the most about was a heavy groaning, and a sound of some person stropping a razor, and for the fear the razor-sharpening might undertake to shave him in his sleep he went away from there.
>
> A few evenings after Arkansas left, a couple of gentlemen were passing the house at about six o'clock and were astonished to see a person they formerly knew in the flesh, but no longer in this world, sitting on the porch reading a newspaper. As they approached the ghost disappeared into the house. They entered the place and found it deserted.

What an amazing story, especially coming from a newspaper article of that era. But there is so much more to add to the story. I researched several books on local desert history and lore, including Bailey's *Golden Mirages*, and the spirit associated with the house in Banner has its own interesting tale to tell.

SONORA JOE

There was a miner who heard stories from the Indians in the desert area of large veins of gold in an area near the Vallecito Mountains. He went by the name Sonora Joe, and the rumors of gold lingered in his mind for many years before he finally made his way to the Anza-Borrego desert. He was searching in these hills for gold when an accident occurred. While crossing a difficult crevasse, his sole pack mule fell, spilling its contents down the hill. Sonora Joe was forced to shoot his wounded animal and had to travel down through the crevasse to reacquire his lost equipment. He discovered that the water canteens had opened in the fall and his only water turned the thirsty sand into mud.

As he was making his way out of the canyon, he noticed a seepage of water from underneath a rock ledge. Filling his canteen with the water from this new found spring, he noticed an outcropping of quartz. Gold runs with veins of quartz at times and Joe somehow managed to forget all his water problems as he grabbed his tools and started to pick at the quartz. After taking out as much quartz as he could carry, he made his way back to his home in Banner to have the samples assayed for gold content. It obviously paid off, for Sonora Joe soon outfitted himself and headed back down to the desert.

After being out in the desert for a couple of weeks, Joe arrived at the Vallecito stagecoach station to rest up before making his way up the hills back to his home in Banner. There Joe boasted about his newfound wealth to one of the locals in the area and mentioned that the one thing he wanted was to get home and hone up his razor for a shave. Sonora Joe never made it home.

The only hint that we have on the fate of Sonora Joe is from a *San Diego Tribune* article dated September 2, 1936:

> A prospector once started from Vallecito for Julian with gold. He never reached there. Years later, the Indians said that some other Indians killed him for his gold and buried the body. Then, fearing discovery, had buried the gold and never recovered it.

When stories in the 1870s of a haunted house in Banner circulated about the sounds of a razor being stropped and scaring off those who lived there, many believed the house was haunted by its previous occupant, Sonora Joe. What I love about this old ghost story is that it has several stories from different sources, both newspaper and oral histories that come together to make one solid tale.

There are many stories like this from the desert, which I believe are there to serve as guardians for hidden gold.

THE EIGHT FOOT SKELETON

There is one story I find fascinating about the Anza-Borrego that I first found in Herbert Lockwood's *Fallout from the Skeleton Closet*. In it, and later in other sources, I found the tale of an eight-foot skeleton roaming the desert with a glow that emulates from the ribs, like its being lit up from the inside.

The story originated during the height of the Julian gold rush and was first reported by an African-American miner who also worked in the town of Julian by the name of Jim Green. Jim was a well-documented character in the history of Julian and was even employed in a livery stable ran by Drury Bailey, Julian's founder. Rumor had it that he was never in want of money and frequently lent money out to those in need.

So how did Jim build his fortune? Not from the livery stable, but apparently from a gold mine he worked, the location of which he kept secret. Many historians of the local gold mines in the area believe Jim may have worked the Phantom Mine, knowledge of which he may have acquired under nefarious circumstances.

The story is there was a Frenchman who came up from the desert to purchase supplies from merchants in Banner. He got drunk and a fight ensued which earned the Frenchman a bullet for his trouble. Jim was there and took care of the man who, perhaps realizing his fate, shared with Jim the location of the mine and asked Jim to deliver the supplies for him. Sometime during the night, the Frenchman expired and his partner came looking for him. When Jim convinced the man to take him on as a porter, they both traveled back down to the mine in the desert. The other gentleman was never heard from again. Jim claimed that he would rather go all the way to Yuma for supplies than go back to Banner because of the violence there, but the truth is Jim probably killed him and he became the sole owner of the Phantom mine. It was Jim who first told of the story of the skeleton haunting the area near his mine to a bartender in Banner.

According to Bailey's *Golden Mirages*, the eight-foot skeleton was once sighted by Charley Arizona. I am not sure if he had any direct connection to Jim Green, but he may have simply been trying to ride the "I've seen it" bandwagon. His tale was miraculous and his description was vivid of the spectral skeleton. I even found a tale of two other miners that wound up embarking on a desert safari hunting the spirit. They even claimed to get a few rounds off and hitting it.

My best theory is that Jim Green invented the eight-foot skeleton as a kind of protector guardian of his mine. No one knows why Jim abandoned his mine; one day he just disappeared. Maybe other people came too close to discovering it. I know that the idea of an unnaturally large glowing skeleton sounds to most modern minds absurd, but to the Victorians, during the height of the Spiritualist movement, it must have seemed terrifyingly real. What better way to keep people from attempting to pillage your mine?

YAQUI WELL

There is another tale of three ghosts that haunt a water source in the area. Yaqui Well, near the town of Borrego Springs is said to be haunted by the

Yaqui Well, Anza Borrego Sate Park.

restless spirits of three immigrants who fought over gold and through madness and murder, paid for their crimes through eternity. The tale told is that the three travelers, crazy from lack of water, ran headlong into the well when they discovered the oasis. One drank far too much water and started to suffer from terrible cramping and died. This can actually happen; the damage done to the body from consuming too much water after starving for water or an extended period can be immense and one can die from shock.

When his companions searched the poor dead fellow, they discovered some gold nuggets he was apparently hoarding. They thought that he must have picked up the gold somewhere nearby and they both became paranoid and decided that they better take the upper hand of the situation. They circled each other slowly around the well until one lunged and they grappled within the muddy well. One gained his balance and grabbed the other by the back of the head and drowned his comrade in the mud-caked hole. The sole survivor clutched the gold and walked into the desert, blind with blood lust. The only witness to this carnage was a local Indian, who watched the story unfold from a nearby cliff.

I love that story—it's a classic campfire story that would run chills down your spine as you snuggled into your sleeping bag at the campground near the well. The story has been around for a very long time and was probably created for the same reason as the eight-foot skeleton. In the desert, water can be just as precious as gold. Protect it any way you can, even with the dead.

GHOST LIGHTS

I cannot let the desert alone without speaking of the ghost lights that are said to inhabit the Anza-Borrego. Many believe that the lights may be the spirits of the dead Native Americans that have yet to find their way home. Others see them as supernatural markers leading to buried treasure. Sadly, some even think of them as a harbinger of impending doom. The first report that I can find of this phenomena is an account of a stagecoach driver in 1858 in which newspapers made an account of these mysterious lights.

Bailey writes of an account of ghost lights by Charles Knowles of El Cajon. He spotted the lights in 1892 while on a prospecting trip with three other men. Shortly after they went to sleep, they were awakened by the shouts of one of the men pointing towards the neighboring mountains. The man claimed he saw a brilliant light on the horizon. They waited some time and claimed that a light about the size of a bushel basket rose slowly up into the air about a hundred feet and then it exploded out, not unlike fireworks. Over the span of around two hours, they spotted two more similar balls of light. Many believe Knowles and his companions did see something out in the desert that night, for there have been similar sightings ever since.

The ghost lights of Borrego appear in different parts of the desert and don't always match the description that Knowles originally gave back in 1892. There have been far too many sightings to simply label them a hoax. Some people believe that the lights are caused by escaping gasses from ore deposits in the area or that it may possibly be a rare occurrence known as ball lightening. Another possible explanation for it may be fireworks used by some for the very *unparanormal* scheme of bootlegging and illegal immigrant trafficking. Another logical possibility is a simple trick of the light caused by tired eyes constantly squinting in the bleak and blinding light of the desert. There are many natural ways to explain these phenomena before we need to delve into supernatural means.

There's a video on *YouTube* that features a fantastic story of how the Anza-Borrego ghost lights proved fatal in 1977. I can only describe it as a faux documentary at best and a complete fallacy at worst. The video goes into detail about John Spreckels, one of San Diego's founding fathers, and the building of the San Diego & Arizona Eastern Railway, dubbed the impossible railroad because of the difficult terrain. According to the video, Spreckel's workers were the first to report the ghost lights, not the stagecoach driver, nearly fifty years earlier. Spreckels became so concerned with the lights and its effect on his men that he hired Pinkerton detectives to investigate the source of the phenomena, to no avail.

It goes on, describing how the mysterious orbs lead people down into the badlands and causes them to get lost, go insane, or even sustain injury. The coup de grace of this video is when they blame the ghostly lights for the derailment of a train which lead to the killing of a brakeman, Benjamin Coe, on the Southern Pacific Railway in 1977, and shows footage of two battered railroad cars lying in the canyon.

I looked throughout the Spreckels file as well as the railway files at the San Diego History Center and could find no mention of this tragedy. But I did find extensive history on the railway itself. According to *Anza-Borrego A to Z*, passenger service was discontinued on the rail line in 1951. Freight traffic continued until September 1976 when Hurricane Kathleen washed out 50 sections of track, destroyed three trestles, and damaged several others, causing it to be shut down for several years, which makes a 1977 derailment impossible. Trains didn't resume running until 1982. There are remnants today of two separate derailments—two boxcars which derailed in 1983 carrying 100-pound bags of cement (those shown in the video) and another boxcar and two truck trailers which derailed in 1963 and were transporting Coors beer. The cargo was retrieved but no lives were lost.

The desert is as beautiful as it is merciless. The natural beauty of the wild flowers in spring makes you forget that you could die quite quickly if you lost your way. Some of the stories I studied go further than the miners and into the mythos of the indigenous people. It's a truly stunning and wonderful place, full of mystery and the spirits of the departed that still have their own tales to tell.

CHAPTER EIGHT

HAUNTING ON THE HIGH SEAS

San Diego is a beautiful coastal city. With a strong tourism industry as well as naval presence, the port is a bustling center of activity. And what would a port town be without a ghost ship? For centuries, ghost ships have captured the imaginations of mariners from the legend of the Flying Dutchman, condemned to sail the seas for eternity, to the real nautical mysteries surrounding the *Mary Celeste* and the *Carroll A. Deering.* Two can be found at the San Diego Maritime Museum. One of the most famous spectral ships around can be found berthed there—the *Star of India*.

STAR OF INDIA

Built in 1863 on Great Britain's Isle of Man, the *Star of India* was originally christened the *Euterpe* and for over thirty-five years sailed under the British flag. It was a fast-moving bark with three masts and boasting a then-modern iron hull. It was used as a cargo ship to carry Indian jute to England as well as Hawaiian sugar to San Francisco. Probably it's most famous duty was transporting emigrants from Europe to Australia and New Zealand. During its time under the British flag, it encountered many mishaps, including several accidental collisions that caused significant damage and one small mutiny that was peacefully averted. In fact, the first captain died on its maiden voyage of scarlet fever. Ship life was dangerous,

Star of India.

Star of India.

and where the passengers and crew lived and worked in such extremely tight quarters, death and dismemberment must have been a somewhat common occurrence.

In 1898, the ship transferred to American hands, was renamed the *Star of India* and spent its remaining active days salmon fishing off the coast of Alaska. In 1923, retired from fishing duty, it was left to decay in Oakland. There, the iron hull rusted and the *Star of India* fell into total disrepair. Saved in 1927 for a mere $9,000, it was purchased by the San Diego Zoological Society, which planned to convert it into some kind of floating aquarium and house the seal and sea lion collections. However, this never came to fruition and the sailing ship sat in San Diego Harbor for some years.

During World War II, the U.S. Navy felt that the masts were too high and posed a danger to low-flying aircraft, so they were forcibly trimmed down. Only through the kindness of donations of concerned citizens, as well as aficionados of the great age of sail, was the *Star of India* able to reach its true glory. In 1976, just in time for the bicentennial, the *Star of India* was restored to its original condition and once again took to the seas. Today, the *Star of India* is the oldest active sailing vessel in the world, going out approximately twice a year.

The flagship of the San Diego Maritime Museum, the *Star of India* serves as a floating museum dedicated to the history of this magnificent ship. When you walk its decks, you can smell the salt air, watch the billowing sails and easily be taken back to the elegant age of sail. If you walk the decks long enough, you may encounter something else. Not only is the *Star of India* known for its fantastical sailing history, it is also known for its ghosts. There are said to be at least three ghosts that prowl the decks of this black-hulled beauty.

A FIRST MATE'S CABIN GHOST

One of the haunts of the *Star of India* can be found in the main cabin. Sometimes I wonder what drives a man to suicide, especially under desperate means. A bullet to the brain or a hangman's rope are quick remedies for someone who feels like they have no way out of their current circumstances. But on December 20, 1875, Captain F. McBarnet could not wait for such a simple exit. According to the story that was passed on to me by the museum staff, McBarnet, an Army officer as well as first-class passenger, attempted suicide by slitting his own throat just four days out of England on the way to New Zealand. He was said to have been drinking heavily before even boarding the ship and several witnesses claimed that he was in a terrible fit of depression.

When he was discovered in his bunk in a pool of blood by one of the crew, he was rushed to the ship's surgeon where efforts were made to suture and bandage him up in order to stop the bleeding. Delirious from both the loss of blood as well his own mental illness, McBarnet was placed in the First Mate's cabin and a watch was established. Someone got lazy, however, and left him alone for a moment. McBarnet tore at his bandages, reopened his wounds and bled out, dying in the First Mate's cabin.

There was a notation made in the diary of one of the passengers on the trip, Mr. John Griffiths, who described the solemn event that took place afterwards:

> It has put a gloomy appearance on the ship. They brought him out of the bunk and put him on the main hatch to wait the inquest. The captain and passengers held the inquest and it was brought in that he was insane when he attempted suicide.
>
> He was sewed up in a piece of sailcloth and buried about hours after death had been pronounced. It was a fearful sight to see the blood all over the place after fetching him out.
>
> The ceremony was very oppressive seeing the sailors and passengers with their hats and caps off and the ship's Captain reading the burial over the corpse before putting it into the water. It put a damper on the whole ship.

There have been many alleged encounters with the paranormal that take place in the First Mate's cabin which many of the staff attributes to the death of Captain McBarnet. In 1998, the educational director of the Maritime Museum was sleeping in the cabin as part of an overnight stay with forty or so fourth grade students from local schools. She reported that she was awakened in the middle of the night by her blankets being ripped off and that she found the once-warm cabin to be filled with a chilling air. She swore that even though she was alone in the cabin, she felt that someone or something was in the cabin with her.

What a great story. When I started my own ghost tour company in San Diego, I approached the Maritime Museum with the intent of including it as part of our list of local haunts. I was given the above story in writing by the museum and it was the story I shared with my guests the entire time we visited the beautiful historic ship. I would take them into the main cabin and show them the First Mate's bunk and spin the tale of Captain McBarnet. I had no reason to question the stories given to me because I didn't get them from any book on ghost stories or website; it was given to me by the museum itself. When I started the research for this book, I wanted to verify the story and get it straight from the source—the Maritime Museum library. What I learned, though, was very different from what I had received years earlier.

Yes, there was an Army Captain named F. McBarnet who did indeed commit suicide on board the *Star of India* while it sailed under the name *Euterpe*. He did cut his throat in his own bunk, but he died in his own bunk. The story from John

Star of India.

First Mate Cabin's,
Star of India.

Griffiths is true as well, describing the disposal of his body to the mercy of the tempestuous seas. The suicide can be found in the book *Euterpe: Diaries, Letters & Logs of the Star of India as a British Emigrant Ship* by Craig Arnold. The rest of the story, however, is pulled from someplace else.

When I spoke to the librarian at Maritime Museum and inquired about the story, he gave me a copy of an oral history taken from a sailor on the *Star of India* in the 1920s while on duty in Alaska. It's the memoirs of Captain Carlson who was, at the time, a mate and doctor onboard the *Star of India*.

Carlson explained that he was awakened one morning and instructed by the Captain to work on a man who had tried to commit suicide by cutting his own throat. He proceeded to mix some hot water with carbolic acid in it and, with five men hold the thrashing man down, cleaned and sewed up the neck. The captain had instructed him to put in "homeward" stitches, which is a type of stitch without regard for the neatness of the work. The Captain believed the man was going to die anyway. But the man did survive and they placed him in a bunk. The next morning though, he went crazy again, tore at his stitches and ripped them open.

According to Carlson, no one else on board would come near the crazed sailor. He was forced to sew him up again with cat gut and regular sewing thread and then wrapped up the neck in bandages. The blood soaked and dried into the bandages, making them hard "as a cast." Fearing that the man would harm himself again, they chained him to a winch. Everyone expected him to die but he lived, and after five days of listening to him rave, they sailed into port, met a U.S. Marshal who received him, and took him to an asylum in Sitka. Carlson's account even goes into detail about how the Marshal's wife cooked for the prisoners and she took a special interest in the crazed man from the *Star of India*. That was the last the crew ever saw of him.

It is easy to assume that the above oral history was mixed with the McBarnet story to make one horrifying ghost story. I believe that the collaboration of the two tales was caused by whoever was working up the stories for the *Star of India*'s annual Halloween event, aptly named "Haunted Star." Over the years, this simple campfire ghost story has gotten wrapped up into the paranormal mythos of the ship. Can the ghost of Capt. McBarnet haunt the *Star of India*? Definitely. But the story that is told about his demise is highly inaccurate.

THE BOATSWAIN'S LOCKER

The next spirit that supposedly haunts the *Star of India* can be found in the bow of the ship, in the chain locker. There is a documented death that took place there in 1909, when it was in use by the Alaska Packers Association and making its way back to Oakland after a long session in the icy waters fishing for salmon. An unknown Chinese fisherman was found crushed under thousands of pounds of anchor chain. No one knows exactly how, though some believe that it may have been his task to guide the chain into position and he lost his balance, causing the chain to pile on top of him.

The crewmembers working the capstan couldn't hear his screams over the loud clanking of the machinery and so over a ton of chain came down upon the poor soul. He was literally crushed to death under the immense weight of the chain. There is some modern speculation that the man was murdered beforehand and then placed into the chain locker, thus allowing the crushing chain to destroy all evidence of foul play. As to the identity of the victim, no one can say. During the height of its time as a fishing vessel, there were as many as 300 men on board and not all were recorded.

Visitors onboard the *Star of India* have reportedly experienced a cold presence in that area of the ship. Cold spots as well as the feeling of another in the room have caused many to believe that the chain locker may indeed carry the spiritual remnants of the crushed Chinese worker.

I love walking the decks of the ship and so easily could spend all day on board the *Star of India*, but more than once I have felt a chilling experience in the boatswain's locker. When on tour with guests, or even by myself, I have felt as though we were not the only presence in the cramped, humid room.

Boatswain's Locker—note the chain size to the left.

Boatswain's Locker, looking down into chain storage hatch.

JOHN CAMPBELL

Probably the most famous spirit associated with the *Star of India* is that of young John Campbell. On April 9, 1884, as the *Euterpe* was pulling out of Glasgow through the waterway known as the Clyde, there was a collision with a steamship named *Canadian*. The sailing vessel pulled into port where some hasty repairs were made and she went under way. During these repairs in dock, three stowaways must have made it aboard. One of them was a Scottish teenager, age 14, by the name of John Campbell. The captain had no choice but to let young Mr. Campbell work off his passage by becoming a member of the crew for the duration of the voyage. The young man knew nothing about working on a ship but became a quick study in the art of seamanship.

On June 26th, Campbell was working high up in the masts overhauling one of the lines when he slipped and fell about 100 feet down to the deck. There are

Chain storage area.

reports in the log entry that he struck several objects on the way down, and when he crashed into the deck, his legs were horribly maimed. He was immediately placed under the care of the ship's surgeon who could do little for the boy and Campbell died three days later, never having regained consciousness.

John Campbell had left life in Glasgow for a new adventure abroad. He may have not even known where the ship was headed and probably didn't care as long as it took him away from the life he was determined to leave behind. According to members of the crew, Campbell was eager to learn the trade he was set to, as well as spending his off hours doing what all 14 year olds do—being a kid and playing with several of the younger children on the decks.

Many caretakers, as well as night watchmen, have reported coming across the spirit of young Mr. Campbell. Some have reported being brushed up against by an unseen force near the mast where he took his fateful plunge to the deck. Some have even come forward to say that they have felt a presence of someone touching their backs, perhaps a friendly game of tag being played in the late hours of the night, where the only other player just happens to have been dead for many years.

THE *BERKELEY*

The *Berkeley* is another ship from the Maritime Museum with its own ghostly past. It was built in 1898 as a ferry boat to transport thousands of passengers across the San Francisco Bay. The *Berkeley* made a name for itself during the 1906 earthquake that leveled San Francisco and set the city afire. The ship and its crew worked tirelessly through the carnage and transported survivors across the bay to safety.

Today, the ferry boat carries the main body of the Maritime Museum's collections, as well as its offices and library archives. The ship looks much today as it did in its nineteenth-century heyday. However, there was an incident which caused extensive damage to the hull of this historic ship, and it seems that a victim of this accident remains to walk the decks today.

It was January 13, 1911. A busy Friday afternoon, the *Berkeley* was carrying passengers from San Francisco to Oakland. As it passed Goat Island, an explosion rang out on the main deck, originating in the gentlemen's toilet. The Captain, J.T. Jones, called down to the Chief Engineer James Peacock, fearing there was an explosion in the boilers. Peacock reported that the engine and boilers were sound and that the explosion did not seem to be mechanical in nature.

The first member on the scene of the accident was James King, a state railroad officer. He was nearly blown off his feet from the explosion and stumbled into what remained of the men's toilet. There he discovered the remains of John G.

Main Mast, where John Campbell fell to his death.

BERKELEY
BERKELEY
GAUGUIN NOW OPEN

Berkeley ferry boat, San Diego Maritime Museum.

Norbom and four others wounded in the explosion. King, assisted by Second Officer Samuel Forsberg, helped the injured out of the wreckage. Pipes burst and caused a mad spray of water across the deck. Some passengers panicked and were calmed by the crew.

The cause of the explosion was later discovered. Norbom was a mining engineer who was carrying with him a bottle of nitroglycerin. Nitroglycerin was used at the time for certain mining detonations. Now whether he had it in a case or in one of his pockets, we don't know. Nor do we know exactly how much he had been carrying, but it must have been significant to cause the amount of damage to the hull that it did.

When I interviewed the librarian of the Maritime Museum, he brought an interesting addition to the story. During the coroner's inquest, Norbom's family insisted that it was not an accident; he wouldn't have carried nitroglycerin and that Norbom had believed he was being shadowed. His widow insisted, instead, that he was murdered and it was a case of mistaken identity. Another man, Edwin Hoffschneider, also died from his injuries. Sadly, we'll never know the truth.

Norbom is believed to be just one of the ghosts that haunts the *Berkeley.* Many who work the floating museum have claimed to have seen the figure of a man and believe him to be the accidental bomber. His presence had also been felt in the area that was once the men's retirement room and toilets, which is now office space for the museum staff.

Seems other spirits may inhabit the decks as well. There is another ghost reported wearing a trench coat and fedora on the upper deck. No one knows who he is or even if he died onboard the vessel. There are also stories of a phantom party that can be heard sometimes on the upper deck, even though no one is there.

The Maritime Museum of San Diego offers a fascinating experience and is an excellent way to spend the day if you love the history of seagoing vessels and other nautical things. Walk the decks, breathe the sea air, admire the exhibits, and check out the gift shop. Just remember, when you walk onto an empty deck or into a deserted room, that you might not be as alone as you think.

VISITOR INFORMATION

THE MARITIME MUSEUM OF SAN DIEGO

1492 North Harbor Drive, San Diego, CA 92101
(619) 234-9153

CHAPTER NINE

DEATH TAKES A HOLIDAY

HOTEL DEL CORONADO

The crisp air blew onto her face as she stared out into the vast ocean, perhaps sensing that a storm was brewing and about to blow inland. She stepped out onto the stairs leading down to beach and put the large caliber handgun up to her head. Alone, and seemingly betrayed, Kate Morgan had run short of options and took the only way out left to her. A single shot rang out in the night and her body dropped onto the stairs. The storm quickly came, covering all of San Diego with a cleansing rain. But an even bigger storm was fast approaching—a media circus like San Diego had never seen before.

Ever since that fateful day in 1892, there have been plenty of theories as to why this tragic figure may haunt her old room and the halls of the luxurious Hotel del Coronado. According to the Hotel, reported paranormal occurrences were swept under the rug until the 1960s when the mainstream media began picking them up and publicizing them. Now, they keep documentation of employee and guest reports, mostly post 1980s, including a Secret Service man who experienced loud noises, flickering lights, billowing curtains, and several sightings of Victorian-clad specters.

The only thing I like more than a good historic ghost story is the mystery that led up to it. At first, it seemed like a slam dunk, the perfect set up for a haunting: A woman checks into the hotel, commits suicide on the grounds, and there is plenty of documentation. But there have been some wild theories bandied about of mistaken identity, blackmail, conspiracy, and even murder. Some aspects of the

ENVIRONMENTALLY
SENSITIVE
PLEASE STAY OFF PLANTS
THANK YOU

Hotel del Coronado.

Hotel del Coronado, Beachside.

The only known photograph of Kate Morgan, taken in Hamburg, Iowa in 1884.

case will forever remain a mystery, but as you peel back the layers of the seemingly straightforward death of Kate Morgan, you'll discover the danger of speculation.

The Hotel del Coronado is arguably the most stunning resort in San Diego. Nestled between the North Island Naval Air Station to the north and the Navy Special Warfare Training Center to the south, it outshines even the multi-million-dollar mansions that dot the peninsula on what is considered one of the top ten beaches in the country. To the locals, the hotel is affectionately referred to as simply "The Del." Originally opening its doors in February 1888, it was the dream of Elisha Babcock and H.L. Story to create a first-class seaside resort in the booming town of San Diego.

For $110,000 in 1886, the investors secured the land lots, built a power plant, and set up a series of water pipelines. The building of the hotel would cost an additional one million dollars and took a year to complete. But when San Diego came onto hard times, John Spreckels saved the hotel and became its sole owner, keeping Babcock on as hotel manager. It has served as a popular vacation spot for royalty and presidents, movie stars and the wealthy elite. If you are a movie buff, you will recognize it as the hotel where Tony Curtis and Jack Lemmon hid out with Marilyn Monroe in *Some Like it Hot.* Now it serves as a wonderful testament to architectural beauty and function, a historic landmark and a classical getaway.

The ghost of the Hotel del Coronado goes by many names, but the most prolific is simply the "Beautiful Stranger." It's a tragic tale of anguish over lost love and suicide that captured the headlines of the local papers for weeks after her death. By examining the reports, as well as a copy of the coroner's inquest, we can attempt to piece together the story of her short time at the Hotel del Coronado and her demise.

On Thursday, November 24, 1892, a beautiful young woman stepped off the late morning train from Los Angeles. She traveled alone, which was unusual for a woman at this time, and carried a single valise. She made a short stop at the Hotel Brewster in New Town, San Diego, and made some inquiries before taking the ferry to Coronado. The ferry terminal back then was close to where the *Star of India* is berthed today and she took the quarter mile trip across the bay. From there, she had to walk to First and Orange Streets, where she boarded the trolley to the Hotel del Coronado.

She arrived at the hotel and checked in under the name Lottie A. Bernard from Detroit, Michigan. Babcock was the manager of the hotel at the time. I have read many theories about the death of the young woman and some even point a finger at Mr. Babcock as the cover-up man, but there is no tangible evidence to support this.

Lottie checked into Room 302 on the third floor, a spacious room by Victorian standards, which overlooked Orange Avenue, away from the beach facing towards the trolley tracks that had brought her to the hotel. I have seen the actual hotel register with her registered name (Lottie A. Bernard) scripted beautifully. Sadly, it isn't in her hand but that of the clerk who signed for her.

That day she befriended one of the many bellmen there, Harry West. During the course of her brief stay, they conversed about several things, including her faltering health and her inquiries for her brother, a Dr. M.C. Anderson. West would later testify at the coroner's inquest and provide many details leading up to her death including her claims that she suffered from cancer of the stomach and another time from neuralgia.

The next day, she spoke to A.S. Gomer, one of the managers on duty at the time, at some length and gave him the same story about her brother and claimed that they had become separated at the train station in Orange, California. She claimed that she had tried to claim her three bags but was denied because she didn't possess the claim tickets. She informed the clerk that her brother had the tags. Throughout her stay, she inquired regularly if her brother had checked in.

Hotel del Coronado; Kate Morgan's room is in the left corner.

When told he hadn't arrived, she would shrug it off and simply comment that he would be there soon.

She took a turn for the worse on the third day and went to the druggist, according to the testimony of T.J. Fisher, a real estate agent who worked out of the drugstore, and asked if he had something to ease her stomach pains. The druggist there suggested that she see a doctor but she dismissed the idea telling him that her brother was a doctor and that he would be joining her shortly. Later that evening, West testified she requested an empty pint bottle and a sponge from a drugstore. He fetched them for her and that was the last he ever saw of Miss Bernard.

On the fourth day, she must have stayed in her room for she was not seen by any of the staff. On the fifth day, there was a bustle of activity surrounding Miss Bernard. She first ordered wine, then later a whiskey cocktail to be sent up to the room by West. He drew a bath for her, and after an hour or so, he helped dry her hair. Gomer became concerned about her increasing expenses at the hotel and, when confronted, the woman suggested that he wire G.L. Allen in Hamburg, Iowa for funds to be sent. Her health seemed to be deteriorating rapidly by this point and some reported seeing her in pain and clutching her stomach.

About five that afternoon, she boarded the trolley back to the ferry and took it to San Diego. She entered Ships Chandlery, a retail establishment, and asked if they sold firearms. The owner referred her to Mr. Chick's Gun Shop on Sixth Street. She approached Mr. Chick and told him she wished to purchase a pistol for a friend as a Christmas present. She settled on an American Bulldog, and after purchasing it, along with some cartridges, he showed her how to load and fire it.

W.P. Walters, a witness in the store at the time, feared that she might try to hurt herself with the gun. The American Bulldog was a mass-produced gun with less than perfect craftsmanship. I easily equate it to the "Saturday Night Special" of its day and age. It almost represented what would become the snub-nosed revolver but it carried only five bullets instead of the standard six due to its large caliber.

The last time Harry West saw Lottie Bernard was outside the hotel, staring at the ocean at around six-thirty in the evening. At about seven, she came down to the lobby and called upon Gomer once more to inquire about her brother. When informed that no word had been received, she walked back up to her room. That was the last time anyone saw her alive.

Electrician David Cone found her body the next morning while he was out "trimming the lights" (which meant he was manually turning off all the electric lights outside on the hotel grounds). He hurried for help, stumbled across the gardener, and then sought out the assistant hotel manager, Mr. Rossier, who was on duty at the time. Rossier immediately went to body and assigned the gardener to cover it and remain there until the coroner arrived. The coroner arrived about an hour and a half after she was discovered. The body was removed and taken to San Diego to Johnson & Company Mortuary at Sixth and E Streets.

Dr. Mertzmann, a surgeon and physician, was allowed to examine the body for thirty minutes, though he did not perform an autopsy. He indicated that the bullet had entered the right side of her skull but noted that there was no exit wound. He guessed it was a .38 or .40 caliber judging by size of the wound, and, due to the lack of exit wound, surmised that the bullet must still be in the brain. It was unknown to the physician at the time that the gun was in fact a .44 caliber. There was no mention of gunpowder residue or burns on the side of her face indicating the close proximity of the shot.

A coroner's inquest was called on November 30th and several witnesses were brought in and questioned in the presence of W.A. Sloane, Esq., the Justice of the Peace and acting coroner on the case. Some of the people questioned were: Harry West, A.S. Gomer, the gardener who watched over the body until the coroner arrived, Dr. Mertzmann, and Mr. Chick. A few others were called in and they were questioned in an effort to establish the chronology leading up to her death. Gomer's testimony was interesting for it added that on the day of her death, a telegram arrived along with a bank draft of $25 from Iowa to pay for Lottie Bernard's stay at the hotel. Gomer also added that they found papers in her room, including an envelope addressed to her in Detroit. The assistant coroner, Stetson, who recovered the body from the hotel also found some pills and burnt papers in her room.

The lack of powder burns or powder residue in the coroner's inquest is what some speculators use as the basis of a murder theory instead of suicide. I cannot explain why it wasn't mentioned at the inquest. It could be that the bullet didn't fire correctly, which would explain the lack of an exit wound and produce mild to less obvious powder burns. If the bullet did indeed fire correctly, I would think that there would be a lot more damage to her skull. Also, due to the rain, any powder marks may have been simply washed away.

Most everything we know about the woman's actions prior to her suicide come from the testimony at the coroner's inquest. But here's where it gets interesting—most of the scandalous rumors and wild accusations that surround the mystery can be directly traced back to the newspaper articles that appeared right after her death. For days, newspaper reports were generated surrounding the death of Lottie Bernard. Who was she? Why didn't anyone step forward to claim the body? Why did she take her own life? And in the absence of answers, the newspapers began to speculate and come up with their own.

The first newspaper article appeared in the *San Diego Union* on November 30, 1892 (the same day as the inquest), and paints an elegant picture of a poor, despondent young woman who claimed to have stomach cancer or heart disease and dramatically ended her life. She was described as ladylike, reserved, and well-educated.

> The lamentable suicide was the despairing act of one suffering from incurable disease, perhaps induced from depression of spirits caused by utter loneliness.

Telegrams of inquiry were sent out to relatives in Detroit and to G.L. Allen, who had provided a bank draft of $25 for Miss Bernard at her request.

On December 1st, after the inquest, a few theories were presented in two articles that appeared in the *San Diego Union* since the identity and cause of suicide were still unknown. The first article mostly recounts the testimony given at the inquest as to her condition and activities. But then the speculation begins. What about the mysterious brother she was always inquiring about who never appeared nor stepped forward after death? The article suggests that the brother was really "a closer relation to this unfortunate woman." The article continues that:

> If he had been her lover and had wanted to rid himself of her, he could scarcely have concealed himself more effectually than he has done.

This is where the belief that Kate had been jilted by a lover originated.

The second article takes it even further, that the victim was betrayed, ruined, and deserted in an interview with an unidentified physician who examined the body, most likely Dr. Mertzmann. Though why this was never included in his testimony at the coroner's inquest is noteworthy. The physician completely dismissed the idea that the victim had stomach cancer since no one under 35 is ever afflicted by it and she hadn't wasted away.

The good doctor goes a bit further and claims that because the symptoms of pregnancy and stomach cancer are identical—great pain in the stomach, sour stomach, and vomiting—she might have been pregnant, though this "cannot be definitely proven without a postmortem examination." He said there were indications that the victim had already borne a child. But he suggests that the victim may have tried to induce a miscarriage because of the dark circles under her eyes and sallow complexion, adding:

> In my opinion, she shot herself in desperation over some love affair.

All that from thirty minutes with a corpse.

The *Los Angeles Times* and the *San Francisco Chronicle* both picked up on this and presented what had been written as fact—that her illness was caused by an attempt to produce a miscarriage and that she had been ruined and deserted.

The most interesting bit comes from the *Chronicle*:

> Public opinion is to the effect that the contradictory stories told by the victim of her own unwillingness to face the world were not true and that a man is connected to the story somewhere.

In the *San Diego Union* dated December 2, 1892, a bellboy claimed that another hotel guest, Joseph E. Jones of Boston, stated that he was on the train with the victim. He said that she was in the company of a "well-dressed gentleman" with whom she quarreled throughout the trip from Denver to Orange. It is important to note that this was hearsay from the bellboy, not actual testimony, nor was Jones ever questioned by authorities. His signature is beneath Lottie Anderson in the hotel register and he left town shortly thereafter for his bungalow in India. Later revelations will contradict this claim that the victim was traveling from Denver, but it established the idea that Bernard was traveling with a man and that they had been fighting.

Then the case took an interesting detour. On December 3, the police were contacted by a Miss May Wyllie who asked for a full description of the body. Even though it was not an exact match, Stetson, who was acting as deputy coroner for the case, took note of it because it was the only inquiry made about the identification of Bernard.

The next day, Elizabeth Wyllie claimed that Lottie Bernard was, in fact, her daughter, Lizzie Wyllie, a bookbinder from Detroit. The newspapers had a field day. Lizzie had apparently left home in the company of a married man identified as John Longfield. She had been terminated from her job and ran off with him five weeks prior, perhaps headed for California. Mrs. Wyllie told the police that relatives would come to remove the remains, but no one ever arrived.

For the next several days, the newspapers ran several articles on the newfound identity of the body at Johnson and Company Mortuary. Just by reading the newspaper articles, I can tell you that the subject of the identity was a mess. But to the public, it explained the train ride from Denver, the overheard arguments, and the poor girl's arrival in San Diego without baggage, money, nor friends.

The December 4th article in the *San Diego Union* also tied the Wyllie girl to G.L. Allen, the man who had wired a bank draft to the hotel for Bernard. According to a telegram received in San Diego from the president of the bank through whic[h] Allen had sent money, G.L. Allen did not know the relatives of Mrs. Bernar[d] [a]nd that her husband was believed to be in Wichita, Kansas. This, combined w[ith] the hearsay claim by Jones, is where the story of Bernard traveling across th[e co]unty with her husband originated.

An added twist to the story appeared in the *San Francisco* [...]icle on

December 5th which detailed the Lizzie Wyllie story. The supposedly jilted wife, Mrs. Longfield, admitted that her husband had been gone for five weeks but claimed that her husband was away at work in Cleveland. Because the newspaper had trouble connecting Lizzie Wyllie to G.L. Allen in Hamburg, Iowa, it was speculated that "the girl and Longfield somehow secured the money by illegal means and that in her fear of discovery of her crimes, the girl killed herself."

Newspaper articles that appeared in Hamburg, Iowa and Los Angeles discounted the Wyllie identity, claiming that a professional gambler named Bernard had recently left Hamburg after claiming that his wife was ill in California and that he needed money to bring her back home. G.L. Allen had gone to school with Bernard in Illinois, had never met Mrs. Bernard, and had sent the bank draft out of charity. The *San Diego Union*, however, discounted Allen's claim and stated:

> On the contrary, it strengthens the opinion that somehow Allen is more deeply interested than to the extent of $25 and has invented the story as a blind. A San Diego man who happens to know Allen says he is a man of some wealth, a sport and a lady killer.

But it wasn't until December 9, 1892 that the body was positively identified as Kate Morgan, also known as Katie Logan, who was working as a domestic servant in Los Angeles. There was a trunk that was left at her former employer's residence ever since the day she left on November 23rd. When the trunk was opened, they found a marriage certificate for Thomas E. Morgan to Kate K. Farmer, dated December 30, 1885. They were married in Hamburg, Iowa by a Reverend W.E. Howe.

An article in the *Los Angeles Times* provided more information from Morgan's employers and trumpeted that it had solved the mystery for San Diego. According to the Grants, Katie Logan had arrived from Omaha, Nebraska two months prior. She had worked as a domestic for two other families before joining the Grant household, once using the name Josie Brown. She claimed that her parents lived near Omaha and that her husband was a gambler. She didn't know what had become of him.

Katie Logan had left on Wednesday, November 23rd, telling her employers that she needed to get some papers signed, but that she would return by the following day to help prepare the Thanksgiving meal. She never returned. The police discovered that all traces of identity within her belongings—names, dates, and addresses—had been destroyed. A lock of hair, photographs of a heavily bearded man and a small child were discovered among her effects. There was also a small tin box with the name "Louisa Anderson" engraved on it. A handkerchief with the same name embroidered on it was found among the items in Room 302 at the Hotel del Coronado.

Now that a positive identity had been made, the newspapers had to tie all the conjecture together. Through various newspaper accounts, they presented that Katie Logan was really Kate Morgan, wife of an Iowa gambler. Tom Morgan (who also may be A.L. Bernard) and Kate must have had a scam going on involving gambling with cards. They fought on the train traveling from Los Angeles to San Diego, and by accounts given, he got off at Orange. She must have continued on to San Diego, which was probably part of their original plan, except that he never showed.

According to the *San Diego Union,* dated December 12, 1892, the burial was paid for by her maternal grandfather, Joseph Wilson Chandler. Chandler had raised Kate after her mother and sister died and she lived with her grandfather until she married Tom Morgan. He simply telegrammed the mortuary and instructed them to bury her and deliver him a bill. No other relative came forward after her death. Two days after the telegram from her grandfather, she was buried at Mt. Hope Cemetery with many attendees to the service, most of them women.

Every book I have come across that covers the ghostly story of Kate Morgan vilifies Tom Morgan and makes Kate Morgan the victim. Tom was a gambler who traveled with Kate, often posing as brother and sister, swindling people across the country. After they arrive in Orange, they quarrel and he leaves her. She heads to San Diego, despondent and deserted by her husband after discovering she is pregnant. So she induces a miscarriage, but realizing he isn't coming after her and she is alone, takes her own life. After the deed was done, Tom disappears.

Nothing though, could be further from the truth.

We may never know or understand everything that happened at the Hotel del Coronado in November 1892. But there is one thing that we know for certain—Kate Morgan is a liar. To the Grant family who employed her, she lied about her name, where she was from and that her parents were still alive. To the employees of the Hotel del Coronado, she lied about her name, where she was from, her medical condition, her brother (Kate's only sibling, a sister, died at age 3), and her baggage.

What if Kate herself was the villain? What if Tom Morgan was never in California? When I originally used to tell this tale to my guests on my tours, I knew there were holes in it. I just thought that those holes were missing chunks of history and all tied up in a neat little bundle in the end. That is, of course, until you come across an excellent book entitled, *The Ghost of the Hotel Coronado: The True Story of Kate Morgan* by Terry Girardot, a living relative of Tom Morg

In July of 2000, Girardot was on a road trip researching his famil. In when he stopped at a library in his mother's hometown of Hamburg gan. the library there, he discovered Alan May's book *The Legend of K* sat Interested in the book solely because Morgan was a family name organ down and started to read. He discovered that he was related t and determined to find out exactly who she was and what led to that fateful night in 1892. He came across the only known photo of Kate Morgan to exist taken in Hamburg, Iowa about 1886. The photo belonged to Dorothy Lyness, Tom Morgan's granddaughter, and with the photo came the family story. The family story can be summed up in a note that Dorothy's mother, Jane Mildred Kerhli, wrote about Tom Morgan, her father, in 1961:

> Thomas Edwin Morgan first married a Kate Farmer in Hamburg, Iowa and they had one child—a boy who only lived a day or so and is buried back of the Church in the lot with my parents. Kate ran away with a step-son of Emily Hope Allen Morgan, who was my father's step-mother. Thomas Edwin Morgan received a telegram about a year after Kate left with Mr. Allen, from authorities at Long Beach, California saying identification showed a woman who committed suicide on a beach there and what should they do with the body? Seems said Mr. Allen deserted her. Dad wired back she left of her own accord and he wasn't claiming the body.

Indeed, an article that appeared in the *San Diego Union* on December 18, 1892, from Hamburg, Iowa corroborates this:

> This town was much surprised on learning that the woman who committed suicide a few days ago in San Diego proved to be Mrs. Kate Morgan of this place. Mrs. Morgan had not been living with her husband for several months.

Seems the "beautiful stranger" wasn't what we all believed her to be—leaving town with another man, heading out west, and leaving Tom Morgan in the dirt. Now whether she left with Albert Allen, the stepson of Morgan's stepmother, can't be proven but she would never see Iowa again. Albert C. Allen was born in 1847 and disappeared off the U.S. Census records by 1870 when he was about 24 years old. But we do know that he had a sister named Elizabeth and a brother named George L. Allen—the same man who wired Kate Morgan a bank draft, who lived in Hamburg, Iowa.

On October 31, 1886, Kate Morgan did give birth to a son also named Thomas E. Morgan but the child only lived for two days. The grave is in the Morgan family plot in Utterback Cemetery in Riverton, Iowa.

Arriving in California, she held down several jobs in just a few months. Using aliases such as Josie Brown, Katie Logan, and eventually Lottie A. Bernard, she makes her way down the southern California coast. Now whether she is traveling in the company of another during this time, we can't say. We do have evidence that she had plenty of money ($1,600) on her when she arrived in California, based on the statements of her uncle, W.F. Farmer, with whom she stayed with in ne d, California briefly before she arrived in Los Angeles. The money was d and what happened to it remains a mystery.

When they checked her items at the Hotel del Coronado after her death, she had $16 on her, enough to pay for her rooms. Why then did she ask to have a wire sent to G.L. Allen back in Iowa for money? When she first arrived in San Diego, she went to the Hotel Brewster (the same hotel where J.W. Collins committed suicide in the Villa Montezuma chapter) and inquired about a Mr. and Mrs. Anderson. When told there were no guests under that name, she went to the Del and checked in under the Lottie A. Bernard alias and informed the staff that she was waiting for her brother, a Dr. Anderson, who never showed. She had no luggage, no clothing except for a nightdress.

We know she had no immediate family and Girard discovered records that prove her husband was in Hamburg, Iowa in 1892. If she did leave Hamburg mired in scandal, had stiffed her employer over the holiday weekend, and lost her money or a man, she had very few options and no one to turn to. It also better explains why no one from Hamburg, Iowa came forward to claim her body.

Tom Morgan lived a happy life after Kate. He remarried in 1893 to Jennie Devor and they spent the rest of their lives together in a small town named Burchard, Nebraska. Tom was listed as a mail carrier in the U.S. 1900 Census, and, in 1907, became the postmaster for the area. They had one daughter, Jane Mildred, and a granddaughter, Dorothy. Thomas Edwin Morgan passed in March 1936, following an illness. His obituary was the summary of a hard-working, respected member of the community who served as Deacon of his local church.

Tom and Jennie Morgan, daughter Mildred and granddaughter Dorothy.

Terry Girardot spent months looking through family records, land deeds, and mortgages, as well as newspaper clippings from all over the west coast and Iowa. His book clearly outlines the coroner's inquest, the newspaper accounts, and his research. What I admire so much about Girardot's book is that he didn't write the book for money or fame. All he wanted to do was clear Tom Morgan's name. By reading all the research, the books, the newspapers, and even the bills of sale for livestock, I am convinced that Tom Morgan had nothing to do with the death of Kate Morgan.

I have read John T. Cullen's book *Dead Move* and he presents a very interesting theory. He believes that there was both Lizzie Wyllie and Kate Morgan and the whole thing was part of an elaborate scheme to blackmail John Spreckels, the owner of the hotel and one of the richest men in the nation. I found his research thorough but I just can't buy into the "Spreckels Machine" conspiracy that he developed to explain how the whole suicide or murder was covered up by the Hotel manager, Babcock and his cohorts and shoved under the rug as fast as possible. By looking at the way the body was splayed on the stairs, as well as the gun, it looks neat the way it is. I could find no proof linking John Spreckels to either ladies.

I honestly believe that after reading the newspaper accounts, Mrs. Wyllie was so desperate to find her missing daughter, she clutched at straws in her identification of the body. But she claimed that her daughter had pierced ears, while the body at the mortuary clearly did not. To Cullen, that's a small oversight, but to me, it's as good an identifier as a birth mark or mole. You either have it or you don't. (On a personal note, even though I don't agree with Cullen's theory, I strongly recommend his book as a great read and very good history piece.)

As for the other players who were vilified by the newspapers, Lizzie Wyllie was found alive and well living in Toronto, Canada. Mrs. Longfield wrote to her husband, John, to "General Delivery" in Cleveland, Ohio and informed him of the newspaper claims. He was indeed in Cleveland and answered that he had just received a letter from Lizzie and that the speculation was false. George Allen, neither a sport nor a lady killer, was prominent in the stock-buying business, moved to Colorado but was buried in Hamburg upon his death in 1924. A letter written by Peter Wikoff defending Allen's upstanding character did appear in *the San Diego Union* on December 24, 1892, stating in conclusion "the San Diego man who says Mr. Allen is a sport and a lady killer, is a coward and is afraid to make the statement over his own signature."

The story of Lottie A. Bernard/Kate Morgan and her ghost has been the inspiration for several books. One of the more interesting books to cover this is Alan May's *The Legend of Kate Morgan: The Search for the Ghost of the Hotel del Coronado.* May wrote this book in 1991, long before the latest ghost-hunting rage came about. May was a criminal defense lawyer from San Francisco who claimed that he located the room that she stayed in through some trial and error, so he could experience the haunting for himself. He thought she had stayed in one room, when in fact she stayed in another. The hotel changed the numbering system of its rooms to better assist guests with finding their rooms and to accommodate the expansion of the hotel. He wrote though, that he got much more than he bargained for. He stated that he saw her face in the television set in the room as well as even dined with her.

I found his claims to be quite humorous at times. May also believed that it was not suicide but murder, noting that there was rust on the gun which shouldn't be on a new gun. Actually, the gun was identified by Mr. Chick *by* the rust on the gun. It was a cheap knockoff and may have been a used gun. Also, the gun may have easily developed a rust patina if it was out in the rain all night and then stored before presenting it to the inquest the next day. May is also responsible for placing the marker on Kate's grave at Mt. Hope which reads, "Kate Morgan also known as Lottie Bernard."

Gravestone of Kate Morgan, Mt. Hope Cemetery.

The book *Beautiful Stranger: The Ghost of Kate Morgan and the Hotel del Coronado* is the official account of Morgan's stay published by the Hotel del Coronado and was written by its heritage department. The book is well researched and addresses the many outlandish falsehoods with clarity and precision. However, because it is primarily an account of Kate's visit to the hotel, it doesn't quite go far enough in the defense of Tom Morgan and the idea that he and Kate traveled the country by train swindling people. The evidence is there that Tom Morgan was a farmer who remained in Iowa during this time, but the book stops at Kate's final identification and doesn't address Tom's involvement.

This illustrates that what is most important about the Kate Morgan case is the evidence that is missing. There is no evidence that Kate was pregnant—it was pure speculation from an exterior examination. There is no evidence that

Tom Morgan was ever in California. To the contrary, there is written record that he was in Hamburg about the time of the suicide. According to a bellboy, one guest said that he saw her on a train from Denver, but it couldn't have been Kate Morgan, who had been working the past few months in Los Angeles.

The newspapers were so desperate to explain why this young woman had taken her life that they presented ideas and theories with absolutely no evidence. She must have been ruined and deserted by a man to have taken her own life. Even when it became obvious that she had lied about virtually everything from the moment she arrived, the opinion remained that a villainous man with ulterior motives must have been behind it—whether it was John Longfield, Tom Morgan, or George Allen. The truth is that the tragic figure of Kate Morgan that you read about today was created by the newspaper accounts and false information given by her to staff at the hotel.

We'll never know where she spent Wednesday night after leaving the Grant house, or what happened to the $1,600 she supposedly had, what papers she needed signed, why she went to San Diego, or who she was waiting for. But we do know she left Iowa, worked in Los Angeles under various aliases, hopped on a train without any luggage, went to the Hotel del Coronado, asked George Allen for money, bought a gun, and killed herself. Why she haunts the hotel, I leave to the reader to decide.

VISITOR INFORMATION

HOTEL DEL CORONADO

1500 Orange Avenue, Coronado, CA 92118
(619) 435-6611

CHAPTER TEN

CEMETERIES & OTHER PLACES WHERE DEAD PEOPLE HANG OUT

Cemeteries certainly have the prerequisite dead bodies for a haunting, but it's important to know that things aren't always as they appear and it's not a guarantee of paranormal activity. Cemeteries are scattered throughout San Diego but, oftentimes, you wouldn't know it. If you wander through Old Town San Diego, you cannot walk more than a few blocks without coming across land that was once part of a cemetery, but no longer. Whether you are in the luxurious neighborhood of Mission Hills, or riding the carousel down in Seaport Village, the restless dead are nearby.

OLD TOWN SAN DIEGO

One of the oldest cemeteries in San Diego, El Campo Santo Cemetery, dates back to 1849 and served as the Catholic cemetery for the early residents of the pueblo that would later be known as Old Town San Diego. When you walk through the roughly quarter-acre cemetery today, it's hard to imagine that is was once almost four times larger than what you see now and home to 477 bodies. The cemetery deteriorated over the years as the city center moved closer to the waterfront and a streetcar later bisected the hallowed grounds. In 1933, the cemetery was restored as accurately as possible based on early photographs and descriptions.

El Campo Santo Cemetery.

But by the late 1950s, only three markers remained, with most carted off by souvenir hunters. An article in the *San Diego Union*, dated August 14, 1957, states that Yankee Jim's grave was unmarked along with many others, including San Diego's first mayor, Don Juan Maria Osuna, and murderer Antonio Garra. Another restoration took place and markers were placed on gravesites which were located by ground-penetrating radar. However, it was impossible to identify who was in the actual graves.

Therefore, new headstones were randomly placed on gravesites. Other markers were placed in the sidewalks and streets around the cemetery. But that is not the only cemetery in Old Town that has seen the ugly face of progress, and El Campo Santo isn't the only cemetery in Old Town known for its ghosts.

Gravesite marker on sidewalk outside El Campo Santo.

The first true cemetery in San Diego was a short walk up the hill to the top of Presidio Park and was in use from 1769 to 1830. Now home to the Serra Museum, this was the site of the first settlement in San Diego, a fort or "Presidio." On the outside of the wall was El Jardin del Rey (The King's Garden), a cemetery for the Spanish soldiers and civilians who came to work at the fort. There was a small church, the first California mission, which several years later would be moved down the hill near fresher water and closer to the indigenous people they were trying to convert.

Before the Spanish came to the hill overlooking the natural bay of San Diego, the Kumeyaay Indians lived there and used the grounds near the top of the hill as a burial ground as well. Even when the Presidio was abandoned in 1835, and people moved down the hill to what is now Old Town San Diego, burials continued at the top of the hill. The last person to be buried in this old cemetery was Henry D. Fitch, a famous sea captain and merchant in the pueblo of San Diego, in 1849. Even though he was Caucasian, Fitch was baptized as a Catholic in 1829, and became a Mexican citizen in 1833 which, at this time under Mexican rule, was a requirement for owning land.

In 1907, George Marston purchased the land on which the Presidio ruins stood and built the Serra Museum, which for many years was used as the headquarters for the San Diego Historical Society. During its construction, the cemeteries for both the Native Americans and the Spaniards were demolished by the construction crews who came and landscaped the hillsides. I have read a story about a spectral white deer that used to wander the grounds in life, and still does in death. When I worked at the Serra Museum, some of my coworkers swore that there was something about the museum that wasn't natural. Perhaps the artifacts housed inside carry more with them than a glimpse into the past. I honestly cannot say.

Serra Museum, site of former Presidio and first cemetery in San Diego.

As part of the historic representation of the Presidio, there is also a partial mock-up of the walls of the old Presidio to give visitors an idea of scale for the Spanish fort. Along one of the walls of this reconstruction is a solitary tower. This tower is a monument to Sylvester Pattie. Pattie, a Kentucky native, was an officer in the War of 1812, and after the war, both he and his son headed west for a new life as trappers. In 1828, he and the members of his trapping party were captured by Mexican authorities and charged with being spies for the Spanish crown. Claiming innocence, the men lingered in a cell in the Presidio awaiting their sentence. I found this narration in a book, *The Personal Narrative of James O. Pattie*, written by the younger Pattie about their experiences:

> I have become so emaciated and feeble that I could hardly travel across my prison floor. But no grief arrests the flight of time, and the twenty-fourth of April came, in which the sergeant visited me and in a manner of mingled kindness and firmness told me that my father was no more. At these tidings, simple truth calls on me to declare, my heart felt relieved. I am a hunter, and not a person to analyze the feelings of poor human nature. My father was now gone, gone where the voice of the oppressor is no more heard.

Sylvester Pattie was the first American reportedly killed on California soil. The tower seen today was actually an Eagle Scout project during the 1960s and is used as storage by San Diego Parks and Recreation for gardening equipment, etc. I am highly amused by certain websites that refer to this shed as The Witches Tower. I was even appalled when I learned that a local tour company was taking guests up there, telling them that it was the old jail for the Presidio in which Pattie was executed and used by the local pagans as a meeting place for ritualistic witchcraft.

There is a small flight of stairs that take you to the top of the tower where there is a five pointed star made out of clay tiles in the floor design. The pentagram, which dates back to ancient Greece, was most likely intended to be an architectural design. True, Wiccans and Neopagans use the pentagram as a symbol of faith but enclose it within a circle, transforming it into a pentacle. The pentagram on the Tower floor is not encircled. Have local pagan groups performed ritual ceremonies up there? Maybe. Is it corny? Yeah, kind of. Is it a Witches Tower? No.

There have been several stories of paranormal activities on the grounds of esidio Park. Apparitions, odd happenings and even the ghostly white deer e been spotted on the grounds of the historic site. The Spanish built a fort hat may have been Native American holy ground. A wealthy philanthropist museum on top of the site where the old fort once stood and completely ed the old cemetery there. It's no wonder that ghosts and other na have been reported on this historic and holy place.

The Presidio Cemetery and later El Campo Santo held the Catholic burials in the pueblo of San Diego, but what about those of other faiths? You needn't look any further than the 5 freeway which runs alongside Old Town. In 1850, Alcalde (Spanish for mayor) Joshua Bean, the brother of the famous Judge Roy Bean, deeded the land to Adolphis Savin who later sold it to Juan Bandini and William Heath Davis. About a month later, the Protestants started to bury their dead there. As the population of Old Town dwindled and New Town became the center of the city, the relatives of the deceased moved their dead to other cemeteries. In time, the land fell into complete misuse and became a garbage dump, a dog pound, and even a goat farm.

In the 1940s, the unearthing of a skeleton brought the original land use to light. Four graves were the only ones that could be identified. One was Frank Ames, Francis Steele, Jack Hinton, and the infant son of Thomas Whaley, Thomas Whaley Jr. The man who owned the land received permission to bury the remains in Mt. Hope Cemetery. Sadly, due to a paperwork error, both Frank Ames and Francis Steele wound up in Potter's Field, the poor section of the cemetery. The land was eventually acquired by the city and completely mowed down to build the 5 freeway. Millions of people drive over the bodies of some of early San Diego's residents every time they travel this portion of the freeway.

The Jews of San Diego received five acres of land as a gift from Louis Rose, a prominent Jewish merchant who arrived in San Diego in 1850. The beautiful stretch of land was in an area near what is now Point Loma and aptly named Roseville. When a newer Jewish cemetery, Home of Peace, was established in the 1890s and in recognition that the 1862 cemetery was no longer in use, the remains were removed and relocated in 1937.

PIONEER PARK

Old cemeteries are often long forgotten and give way to progress. But what happens when sheer neglect takes hold? That's what happened to Pioneer Park, or as it used to be known, Calvary Cemetery. In 1870, the city set aside ten acres of land to be used as a cemetery in the area now known as Mission Hills. Half of the cemetery would be reserved for Catholics, the other half for Protestants. The Protestants never claimed their half and Calvary Cemetery was born, the final resting place for some 1,650 souls.

When Holy Cross Cemetery, which is located several miles to the east of Downtown, opened in 1919, Calvary fell into disuse. A wall was built around the cemetery, but vandals still came in, ruined tombstones, and held parties into the long hours of the night. The caretaker's shack caught fire one year, thus destroying a huge portion of burial records as well. There were occasional burials up into the 1960s, but it was exceedingly rare. In 1968, the Roman Catholic Bishop filed

Sylvester Pattie Memorial a.k.a. "Witches Tower."

a quitclaim on the cemetery, thus giving the land to the city. Any descendants with relatives buried there could have them moved to Mt. Hope free of charge, for it was a city-owned cemetery.

In 1969, all granite and stone markers that could no longer be read were recycled by Clemens Granite Works, so tombstones would be reduced to fillers for other projects. Some of the memorial stones that were still legible were moved to Mt. Hope, where a small area was set aside for them in a ravine near the trolley tracks that cut through the cemetery. In the park itself, the rest of the stones were placed in the back corner as a memorial to the history of the

Grave marker memorial at Pioneer Park.

old Calvary Cemetery. The cemetery itself became Pioneer Park, with paved walkways and eucalyptus and pepper trees scattering the grounds for shade and beauty.

What about the graves? Well, they never left. They rest below the grass and the playground equipment that adorns this upscale park. Next to the park is Ulysses S. Grant Elementary School. If you ever go there in the evening, wait until the grass has just been watered or the evening dew has settled. You can look down and see where the ground gently drops as the graves settle into the earth as the years go by.

CASSEN

ark.

Grave marker memorial

ker memorial at Pioneer Park.

There have been many different groups interested in paranormal investigations at Pioneer Park. I have heard and read plenty of stories of ghostly lights around the converted cemetery which remind me of Will o' the Wisps, spectral lights that wander the countryside and places of the dead. These ghostly lights heavily influenced the jack o' lantern mythos. Knowing a lot about these ghostly lights, I honestly believe that they may be caused by the escape of methane gas, which can happen with the decomposition of bodies. But there has been a lot more phenomena reported there than just spectral lights, so perhaps something else resides amongst the grassy hills of this lush park.

DEAD MAN'S POINT

Sadly though, there is one old cemetery, in fact San Diego's oldest, that almost no one knows about. It was called Dead Man's Point. In 1782, two ships were outfitted with supplies and courageous settlers and made their way up the Alta California coast. The *Princesa* and *La Favorita*, sailed under the command of Captain Juan Pantoja y Arriga, and were the victims of bad luck throughout the entire voyage. Of the roughly 300 men who came to settle into upper California, a third of them died from disease, scurvy, and dysentery. As the ships pulled into the first accessible harbor, the bodies were taken off the ship and simply laid to rest in the swampy area near the makeshift anchorage. That small landmass is still there today and is now the famous tourist shopping center, Seaport Village. Underneath the shops and beautifully restored carousel, lies the many dead who didn't survive the voyage here. Ironically, Juan Pantoja y Arriga has a park built that bears his name on G Street and Columbia, complete with a bronze statue of the explorer himself, not too far from the remains of his crew.

Memorial marker for Dead Man's Point.

CONCLUSION

Legend: A lie that has achieved the dignity of age.

~H.L. Menkin
Twentieth century journalist and philosopher

It's interesting that in this age of information, it's no longer enough to just experience paranormal phenomena and say we've had a brush with the Other Side. If a vase falls off a shelf or we suddenly feel a chill or we catch a glimpse of a figure out of the corner of our eye or see an impression on a just-made bed, it's not enough to accept these occurrences. We then feel the need to know why—to attribute the phenomena to something or someone. The impression in the bed is deep, so it must be a man. A man once owned this building and died here so his spirit must still linger; but why? He must be upset or perhaps even unjustly wronged. A story is then woven around the experience.

These historic ghost stories have a habit of becoming more and more convoluted even though there is no evidence to support them. Often there is the addition of more tragic deaths attributed to the site again without any physical evidence of human existence. Are they simply reasons to justify the presence of paranormal activity? Why do we persist in believing and perpetuating these stories when presented with a glaring absence of evidence, confessions of fabrication, implausibility, or even physical evidence to the contrary? Aren't all ghost stories then susceptible to being tarred with the same brush?

Marcello Truzzi, a professor of sociology and co-founder of the Committee for the Scientific Investigation of Claims of the Paranormal, once said, "Extraordinary claims require extraordinary proof." Perhaps these legends are created or embellished by those compelled to explain the paranormal activity encountered in an effort to believe, or because they're afraid of, what they do not understand.

The origins of these ghostly legends are of particular interest. It is not unusual to find a newspaper report of strange paranormal activity dating back to the late nineteenth century when the country was at the height of Spiritualism. When evaluating these paranormal legends, therefore, it becomes relevant to know if there is a history of ghosts being reported on the premises.

For example, there is a newspaper account from 1874 about a small house in the San Diego backcountry which was reported to be haunted. Sadly, the house is no longer standing. The Villa Montezuma had a reputation as "a house built for spooks" back in 1913. But compare that to the Horton Grand Hotel whose infamous ghost can only be traced back to 1986, when the hotel was refurbished, re-opened, and in need of business, and the story becomes dubious.

There are thousands of books and websites out there that cover the local mythos and spin horrific tales of specters and phantasms that roam the sites of their demise. I love them all, my bookshelves are filled with them. These campfire stories usually fall into two categories: folklore which is made up of legends, oral histories, and cultural traditions—and fakelore, which purposely manipulates history and the facts surrounding this history for the sole purpose of making the tale more interesting.

Folklore is ingrained in our culture and heritage, adds charm and romanticism, and reminds me of a bygone age. The stories covered in the desert are excellent examples of folklore—they are tales that have been told for over a century. Some of the tales indeed can be viewed as outlandish musings of miners and explorers or visions of sun-stroke victims, but others are deep rooted in the history of the region.

Associating spirits, gods, or paranormal guardians with gold, hidden treasure, or wealth is likewise an ancient and universal tradition. In Egypt, shrines were specifically built near gold mines. Sanctuaries of Hathor, who was responsible for the success and well-being of the mines, have been found at Timna and other sites. In Greek mythology, the griffin was a monster with the body of a lion and the head and wings of an eagle. They would find gold in the mountains and build their nests upon it and kept vigilant guard to prevent its discovery from unworthy seekers. In English folklore, it is said that demons guard King Richard II's gold in a well at Beeston Castle and ensure that anyone trying to reach it will go mad or be stricken dumb with horror. Wherever you find a story of a lost mine, buried treasure, or potential riches, you'll find supernatural forces in the vicinity.

Fakelore is a slippery slope because not only is it cleverly disguised as folklore to add authenticity, but it eradicates the true history of the story it mimics. These stories appear to be historic in nature but without a shred of validation to support their claims. They can create people who never even existed, alter family histories, and create misconception.

The fakelore of Roger Whitaker, covers up the richness of a boutique hotel with a wonderful historic past. His story is plausible—a gambler gets caught cheating the wrong guy and ends up with a bullet in his belly. He stumbles back to his hotel room, crawls in an armoire, is found, and killed. But there is no record of Roger A. Whitaker in San Diego. The only evidence of his existence is in 1986 when he communicated telepathically with a rent-a-psychic.

Kate Morgan's story began as folklore. The well-known history of her suicide and the mixture of conjecture makes one tantalizing story that would make any seeker of the macabre want to pony up the money for the room in which she stayed. Unfortunately, fakelore gets mixed up in this when you read about how her husband Tom was a gambler and family histories were forever altered. The newspapers wrongly painted a picture of a pregnant woman, deserted by her callous husband, who tragically took her own life. Tom Morgan, John Longfield, and George Allen were all victimized by the media sensation that Morgan's suicide created. They were portrayed as villains responsible for the death of a young woman. History shows us quite the opposite but people will simply seek out and regurgitate the story that they find more interesting, whether it's true or not.

Gross misconceptions are also created by fakelore. The town of Julian has had to contend with the belief that there were two cemeteries in their tiny town—one for blacks and one for whites. As Julian historian David Lewis stated, maybe some people can't accept that in a post-Civil War environment, people of all races could work, live, and die together. The town was a melting pot and business owners, miners, and farmers came from all walks of life. It was a lively close-knit community filled with Saturday night dances, midnight buffets, festive 4th of July celebrations, mining camp rivalries, and award-winning agriculture. There is one cemetery and it is filled with every kind of nationality.

"The Ballad of Yankee Jim," written in 1966, created the misconception that Yankee Jim was unjustly convicted of the petty theft of a rowboat. The claim that he was unconscious during his three-day trial, the judge was drunk, and the townspeople just wanted blood is completely unsubstantiated. No wonder he haunts the Whaley House, claimed an actor who performed in the drama. Of course, the fact that Yankee Jim confessed to the crime as well as admitted to stealing horses on his way down from Stockton is swept under the carpet. Never let the facts get in the way of a good story.

I recently read a wonderful book on a historical murder spree that happened locally in the 1860s. The author, William Lawton Wright, a past director of the San Diego Historical Society, wrote a very enlightening statement about the problems of hearsay:

> Remembered hearsay is not knowledge; it is a chain that weakens and kinks with every added link, or generation. In a few decades the legendry of a region is only its most stubborn opinions, right or wrong. The truth may have been crushed by accumulative errors.

An example of this is the Whaley House where, in my investigation, I had the opportunity to interview several of their docents. I had the opportunity to interview a staff member who insisted that "Thomas Whaley had to be at the hanging of Yankee Jim and that not all history is documented." True, but as you read earlier, Whaley was quite the prolific letter writer, averaging several per week. His personal letters make no mention of the event, even one written the day after the hanging. This "fact" was created simply by the word of mouth and retold over and over again in books and internet websites.

I hope you came to the same conclusion as I did when you read the stories of these famous historic haunts: Truth is indeed stranger than fiction. Thomas Whaley gave us a glimpse into life in early San Diego, suffered personal tragedies, yet left behind a house that is quite possibly haunted, but certainly not certified as such by the U.S. government. Kate Morgan was an accomplished liar who most likely ran off with her husband's stepbrother in scandal. Jesse Shepard was an accomplished, internationally celebrated musician and author who died in abject poverty in Los Angeles.

Pursue legend and you are left mystery mongering and clutching for the truth in a web of fiction and sometimes blatant lies. Dig deeper and uncover the truth, and no one truly loses. The stories become more interesting, and then you truly appreciate the historic site for what is. If you take this book as a primer for investigating the paranormal of this city, then you are better armed than most. As you stay awake into the late hours of the night, attending vigils in hopes of contacting the dead not able to pass on, at least you will know their true names and possibly what doomed them to their fate.

BIBLIOGRAPHY

Bailey, Phillip A. *Golden Mirages*. New York, NY: Macmiliian Publishing Co., 1940.

Belanger, Jeff. *The World's Most Haunted Places*. New York, NY: Fall River Press, 2004.

Bishop, Greg. *Weird California*. New York, NY: Sterling Publishing Co., 2006.

Cullen, John. *Dead Move; Kate Morgan and the Haunting Mystery of Coronado*. San Diego, CA: Clocktower Books, 2008.

Girardot, Terry. *The Ghost of the Hotel del Coronado: The True Story of Kate Morgan*. Dallas, Texas: DME Creative Services, 2001.

Holzer, Hans. Ghosts: *True Encounters with the World Beyond*. New York, NY; Black Dog & Leventhal Publishers, Inc., 1997.

Hotel del Coronado Heritage Department. *Beautiful Stranger: The Ghost of Kate Morgan and the Hotel del Coronado*. San Diego, CA: Hotel del Coronado, 2005.

Botts, Myrtle. *History of Julian*. Julian, CA: Julian Historical Society, 1969.

Lamb, John J. *San Diego Specters*. El Cajon, CA: Sunbelt Publications, 1999.

Lewis, David. *Last Known Address: The History of the Julian Cemetery*. Julian, CA self published, 2010.

Lockwood, Herbert. *Fallout from the Skeleton's Closet: A Light Look at San Diego's History*. San Diego, CA: San Diego Independent, 1968.

MacPhail, Elizabeth C. *When the Red Lights Went Out in San Diego*. San Diego, CA: San Diego Historical Society, 1974.

May, Alan M. *The Legend of Kate Morgan: The Search for the Ghost of the Hotel del Coronado*. Colchester, VT: Elk Publishing Inc., 1991.

May, Antoinette. *Haunted Houses of California*. San Carlos, CA: Wide World Publishing/Tetra, 1990.

Taylor, Troy. *Ghosts by Gaslight*. Decatur, IL: Whitechapel Productions Press, 2007.

Wlodarski, Robert and Anne. *Haunted Whaley House II*. West Hills, CA: G-Host Publishing 2004.

Wlodarski, Robert and Anne. *Bottles of Boos*. West Hills, CA: G-Host Publishing, 2006.

Wlordarski, Robert and Anne. *California Ghosts*. West Hills, CA: G-host Publishing, 2007.

White, Gail. *Haunted San Diego: A Historic Guide to San Diego's Haunts*. San Diego, CA: Tecolote Publishing, 1993.

ACKNOWLEDGMENTS

Through the writing of this book, I came across some great and knowledgeable people. I wanted to give special thanks to the following:

Sean Shiraishi, Gina Petrone, David Lewis, Molly McClain. I would also like to thank the staff of the San Diego History Center and the Julian Museum for their time in helping me compile the research for this book.

AUTHOR CHARLES L. SPRATLEY AT JULIAN PIONEER CEMETERY.

ABOUT THE AUTHOR

Charles Spratley, a native of San Diego, is an accomplished historian, having worked for both the San Diego Historical Society and Save Our Heritage Organization (SOHO) as a docent/site interpreter for several prominent historic properties and sits on the Board of Directors for the Friends of the Villa Montezuma. He founded a local ghost tour company, lectures at the university level on Roman and Greek history, and has appeared in local media (both television and print) speaking on ancient lore, superstitions, and the paranormal. Spratley has a teaching credential in hospitality, tourism, and recreation, and currently conducts historic tours throughout San Diego and Orange County.